The Emerald Isle

The Emerald Isle

Basil Hood,
Arthur Sullivan and
Edward German

MINT EDITIONS

The Emerald Isle was first published in 1901.

This edition published by Mint Editions 2021.

ISBN 9781513281421 | E-ISBN 9781513286440

Published by Mint Editions®

MINT
EDITIONS
minteditionbooks.com

Publishing Director: Jennifer Newens
Design & Production: Rachel Lopez Metzger
Project Manager: Micaela Clark
Typesetting: Westchester Publishing Services

CHARACTERS

The Earl of Newtown, K.P. (Lord Lieutenant of Ireland)
Dr. Fiddle, D.D. (his Private Chaplain)
Terence O'Brian (a Young Rebel)
Professor Bunn (Shakespearean Reciter, Character Impersonator, etc.)
Pat Murphy (a Fiddler)
Irish Peasants:
    Black Dan
    Mickie O'Hara
H.M. 11th Regiment of Foot:
    Sergeant Pincher
    Private Perry
Sentry
The Countess of Newtown
Lady Rosie Pippin (her Daughter)
Molly O'Grady (a Peasant Girl)
Susan (Lady Rosie's Maid)
Peasant Girls:
    Norat
    Kathleen
Chorus of Irish Peasants and Soldiers of 11th Regiment of Foot

ACT I.—Outside the Lord Lieutenant's Country Residence.
ACT II.—The Caves of Carrig Cleena.
PERIOD.—About a Hundred Years Ago.

PUBLISHERS' NOTE: The numbers of the Opera composed by Arthur Sullivan, with the exception of Nos. 1 and 2, which were completed by him, have been orchestrated and harmonized by Mr. Edward German.

Act I

Scene.—*The scene is outside the park gates of the Lord Lieutenant's country residence. Blind Murphy's cabin at side. The stage is empty.*
   Peasants, men and girls, enter gradually, and gather one by one.

No. 1. Opening Chorus.
(Arthur Sullivan)

Girls: Have ye heard the brave news that is goin' around?
Men: Do ye mane that Blind Murphy's owld pig has been
      found?
Girls: Sure, it's better than that what ye mane, I'll be bound
Men: Are ye spakin' of Terence O'Brian at all?
Girls: And it's Terence has sent us a warnin' to say
      He is secretly coming among us to-day,
Men: And the Saxons may send us to Botany Bay,
         But it's Ireland that's ready to answer his call!
All: For it's Terence they tell has an elegant style,
      And there's not a colleen but would die for his smile;
      He's the red-hottest rebel in all of this Isle,
         And that's why we're howlding this open-air ball!
The men and girls take partners and dance. After short dance.
Girls: Now be aisy wid taisin'
         And squazin'
         And sazin'
      My waist wid your arm like a bundle o' hay!
         It's meself that is dressed
         In my best
         And distressed
      To be tumbled and pressed in that impudent way.
Men: Now be aisy wid taisin'
         Is squazin'
         Displazin'?
      It's wasted the arm that is empty to-day!
         It's meself that is dressed
         In my best
         And distressed

To be tumbled and pressed to keep out of your way!
Will I bid ye good-day?
GIRLS: Now be aisy wid taisin'!
Is squazin'
So plazin'?
MEN: Sure now, my hat I'll be raisin',
And walkin' away!
GIRLS: Now be aisy wid taisin'!
MEN: Acoushla mavourneen, acoushla macrae!
GIRLS: If you're hat you'll be raisin' and walkin' away,
Now, sure it's meself will not stand in your way!
Enter Terence.

No. 2. RECITATIVE.

TERENCE: My friends!
NORA: A Saxon stranger!
TERENCE: No, mavourneen!
I am an Irishman, and love my country,
Though to my shame, I speak with English accent!
For as a baby I was brought to England,
Brought up and educated there—at Eton
And Oxford University. But lately
Have I come back to Erin; only lately
Has that Andromeda learnt to regard me
As her Perseus!
ALL: You are?
TERENCE: Terence O'Brian!
Rebel or patriot—which will you call me?
ALL: Hooroo for you! Here's to you, Terence, darlin'!

No. 2a. SONG.—TERENCE with CHORUS.
(Arthur Sullivan)

TERENCE: I'm descended from Brian Boru,
CHORUS: Hooroo!
TERENCE: My blood is the elegant hue,
CHORUS: True blue!
TERENCE: That colours the veins of the fortunate few

Who are sons of the Kings of Erin!
And whenever a Saxon Viceroy comes
    To Ireland's shore
    With cannons' roar
    And fifes and drums
    And flags galore,
Who'll join in the Saxon cheerin'?
CHORUS: Who? Who?
TERENCE: Not I, for one,
  The worthy son
    Of Brian Boru!
CHORUS: Hooroo for you!
TERENCE: But as he would have done
  My father's son
    Will do!
CHORUS: Hooroo
    For Brian Boru!
    And you,
ALL: Bowld Rebel O'Brian!
TERENCE: Now if Brian Boru were about—
CHORUS: We'd shout!
TERENCE: The Saxon invader he'd flout—
CHORUS: Rout out!
TERENCE: And such importations in future no doubt
    He would put a restrictive tax on!
  So if ever a Lord Lieutenant comes
    To Ireland's shore
    With cannons' roar
    And fifes and drums
    And flags galore,
Who'll help to get rid of the Saxon?
CHORUS: Who? Who?
TERENCE: Well I, for one,
  The worthy son
    Of Brian Boru!
CHORUS: Hooroo for you!
TERENCE: For as he would have done,
  His father's son
    Will do!

CHORUS: Hooroo
    For Brian Boru!
    And you,
ALL: Bowld Rebel O'Brian!

TERENCE (*to Nora*): And now, mavourneen, you will not again mistake me for a Saxon, will you? (*To others*) It is an ever-burning shame to me that I do not speak with the brogue which is my birthright. More—it is an ever-burning injustice! For had not the grasping Government of England purchased my father's dilapidated estate, to serve, after extensive repairs, as a summer residence for their Viceroy, my parents would not have been lured to the luxurious lap of London, where I, their child, was taught by alien nurses to lisp a tyrant tongue! Within those gates lies my father's fine estate, wrested from him by the tempting offer of a rapacious Government!

ALL: Shame!

TERENCE: There rise my father's chimneys, soiled with Saxon smoke, fouled by the fuel that prepares the banquets of a Saxon Viceroy!

Enter Murphy.

ALL: Shame! Shame!

MURPHY: May I speak to your honour?

TERENCE: My honour is my countrymen's. If you are a countryman—

DAN: Devil a doubt! Blind Murphy's never seen a town!

MURPHY: And it's Blind Fiddlers we've been from father to son for more generations than I can remember. But it's ourselves (*who ought to be your tenantry*) that share the injustice with you in the matter of the brogue, or the want of it. It's the Lord Lieutenant forces us to speak Irish with an English accent.

TERENCE: Is it possible?

MURPHY: It is that. For what with his free classes for English Elocution and Deportment, it's the Irish brogue and other characteristics that he tramples under his feet by settin' his face against 'em!

ALL: Bad cess to him!

No 3. SONG.—MURPHY and CHORUS.
(Arthur Sullivan)

Of Viceroys though we've had
    A rather large assortment,

There's never been
One half as keen
As this one on Deportment.
It is the ruling fad
That marks his constitution!
Deportment, and,
You understand,
The Art of Elocution!
And will a man stand tamely by
While Irish jigs are put down,
Because a Viceroy thinks it low
To kick your heels up so—and so—?
Ireland, kick your heels up high,
To show you've put your foot down!
CHORUS: Ireland, kick your heels up high, etc.
MURPHY: Now every Irish boy,
And all colleens (*or lasses*),
Professors teach
The Saxon speech
At Elocution classes!
And all who don't employ
The purest English accent,
Are as a rule
To Infant School
Incontinently back sent!
And will a man be meek and dumb,
And see the Irish nation
Advance by rapid leaps and hops
To be a race of Saxon fops?
Ireland, that's what ye'll become
Wid all this education!
CHORUS: Ireland, that's what ye'll become, etc.
MURPHY: And will a man stand tamely by
And be of brogue bereft now,
Because a Lord Lieutenant's fad
Has made him education mad,
And every boy's alas! a lad
That's taught to read and write and add,
However poorly born or clad?

But being blind myself it's glad
I am that I have never had
To read or write, and now, bedad!
There's only one thing I can add—
Ireland! hold your Rights—and, why,
    Your Rights are all that's left now!

CHORUS: Ireland! hold your Rights, etc.

TERENCE: But why attend the Elocution and Deportment Classes?

MURPHY: Sure, it's the filthy money-prizes that sap the resolution out of a man, and put the correct English into him!

TERENCE: I see.

DAN: It's myself that has had roast pork for a month from the "Boy who stood on the Burning Deck," and the second prize he took with bein' elegantly recited.

TERENCE: But this is monstrous! Do you mean to say that under this alien's influence you have learnt to forget the marked characteristics of our nation?

MURPHY: Your honour, there's not a man nor a colleen here that could dance an Irish jig correctly, and say "Begorra" at the end of it with any conviction. (*Exit*)

TERENCE: Terrible! It shall be my first care to restore and foster these customs. But how? Where shall I find a tutor where all are ignorant?

Professor Bunn has entered; he carries a large carpet-bag.

BUNN (*to Terence, presenting hand-bill*): Permit me!

TERENCE (*reading*): "Professor Bunn."

BUNN: Of Bath.

TERENCE: "Mesmerist, Ventriloquist, Humorist, and General Illusionist." Really, my dear sir, I don't see—

BUNN: You will, sir—you will!

TERENCE: "Shakespearean Reciter, Character Impersonator, and Professor of Elocution. Children's parties a speciality."

This is a political meeting, Mr. Bunn—not a children's party.

BUNN: Sir, in politics or business I favour no particular party.

TERENCE: This is a secret meeting, sir.

BUNN: A lucky meeting, sir—I was on my way to the Lord Lieutenant.

TERENCE: I will not deprive him of your company. I desire nothing in common with the Lord Lieutenant.

BUNN: Don't be hasty, my dear air. I overheard your speech, and I must say your delivery is very fine—very fine indeed. May I ask, are you in Parliament?

TERENCE: Not yet.

BUNN: I thought you couldn't be. Now, sir, I overheard your wishes with regard to the instruction of the Irish peasantry. I overheard your aspirations—you aspirate beautifully—and I said to myself, "That's the man for my money!" or rather "That man's money is for me!"

TERENCE: I don't understand you?

BUNN: I have been engaged by his Excellency the Lord Lieutenant as Local Professor of English Elocution in the Infant Schools. But how would it be if the Character Impersonator of Irish Types were in your pay, eh?

TERENCE: I don't see—

BUNN: You shall see, sir. You want these poor peasantry to be typical Irish, do you not?

TERENCE: It is one of my dearest wishes.

BUNN: It will work out one of your cheapest, if you engage me, I assure you.

No 4. SONG—BUNN, WITH CHORUS.
(Arthur Sullivan)

BUNN: If you wish to appear as an Irish type
  (Presuming, that is, you are not one),
  You'll stick the stem of a stumpy pipe
   In your hat-band, if you've got one.
  Then no doubt you're aware you must colour your hair
   An impossible shade of red;
  While a cudgel you'll twist with a turn of your wrist,
   Being careful to duck your head—
Or your own shillelagh unhappily may accidentally knock you down
With a fearful crack on the comical back of your typical Irish crown!
If you manage instead of the back of your head to belabour the
  floor like that—
And shout "Whirroo," bedad, you'll do! You're the popular type of
  Pat!

CHORUS: Or your own shillelagh, etc.

BUNN: For the innocent joys of a ball or wake
　　　　You probably foster a passion,
　　　For all such things I can undertake
　　　　To teach the latest fashion.
　　　First you kiss a colleen, then imbibe some potheen,
　　　　Then your coat on the floor you'll trail,
　　　And invite the best man in the room if he can
　　　　To tread on its tattered tail—
　　With a big shillelagh some truculent neighbour will probably
　　　knock you down
　　With a frightful fearful crack on the comical back of your typical
　　　Irish crown!
　　At a ball or a wake it's yourself that'll take little notice of that
　　　at all!
　　It's used you'll get to the strict etiquette of a typical Irish ball!
CHORUS: With a big shillelagh, etc.

DANCE.

TERENCE: Well, Mr. Bunn, I shall engage you.
BUNN: Thank you, sir. (*Gratified*)
TERENCE: Not because I think you will be any use, for your methods
　　seem to me to border on burlesque; but because, having forced
　　yourself into our secret meeting, it would be necessary by the rules
　　of our society to exterminate you if you were not promptly made
　　one of us. Henceforward you will be a member of the Clan-na-
　　Gael. It is the only way to insure your life.
BUNN: I see—a rather heavy premium, but—I see.
TERENCE: I'm glad you do. You will go through the ceremony of
　　initiation and branding at our midnight meeting. (*To others*)
　　Where shall we hold it?
DAN: At the caves—the Caves of Carrig-Cleena. It's a lonely place.
TERENCE: Very well. Go there at once. I will find the way and follow
　　in an hour. You can trust this gentleman to me. (*Showing pistol*)
　　Let the password be "Erin-go-bragh."
ALL: Erin-go-bragh!
BUNN (*feebly*): Erin-go-bragh'
Exeunt all to reprise, except Terence and Bunn.
TERENCE: Mr. Bunn!

BUNN: Sir!

TERENCE: I have no wish to confide my love affairs to you—but—

BUNN: Go on, sir. I'm a bachelor myself.

TERENCE: But there is no help for it. I am in the anomalous position of being secretly engaged, though a rebel, to the daughter of the Lord Lieutenant. I am now going to try to obtain a secret interview with the lady I love—the question is, what shall I do with you?

BUNN: Oh, don't mind me, sir. (*Going*)

TERENCE: It's the question of how to mind you that troubles me. Ah!

Enter Murphy.

Blind Murphy—it would be absurd to ask you to keep an eye on this gentleman—but (*taking a halter from side of cottage, and placing noose round Bunn's neck*) *keep your hand on him—so.*

(*Giving end of cord to Murphy*) *The cord will not slip over his head* (*trying noose*)*, and if he tries to slip over the bridge—*(*to Bunn*) *but I think I can trust you.*

BUNN: I think you have trussed me.

TERENCE: I have a contempt for that form of humour, sir!

BUNN: And, dash me, if I admire yours, sir—dash me if I do!

Exit Terence through park gates. Bunn cautiously produces a large knife and is about to cut the cord.

MURPHY: What are ye doin' with that knife?

BUNN: I am going to cut my hair. For a blind man, you are extremely inquisitive.

MURPHY: I'm not blind at all.

BUNN (*scrutinizing him*): Do you mean to say you are an impostor— that you have been deceiving people all your life?

MURPHY: Only since I left school, when my father taught me blind-fiddlin'—the only honest trade he knew. You're the first I've undeceived, so ye needn't complain. Listen! It's you that shall cure me of my blindness. It's a great little Quack Doctor ye shall be, and restore my sight—the easiest thing in life, seeing I was never without it. The fame of your miraculous cure will spread through the land like the potato disease. It's not money you'll want, but the room to stack it.

BUNN: It's worth considering. But if you have never been blind, why do you want to be cured?

MURPHY: Look down the road. What do you see?

BUNN: A colleen. As far as I can tell, a sweetly pretty young person.

MURPHY: That's why I want to be cured. It's this way: how can I tell she's sweet and pretty while I'm blind? How can I tell her how she looks, and how can I ask her to look at me, if I'm blind?

BUNN: You couldn't do it, of course.

MURPHY: Of course not. And how can I tell her I've never been blind without sayin' I'm a mean, deceivin', thievin' hypocrite, that's been stealin' her pity under false pretenses? A miraculous cure is my only remedy, and it's you that shall supply it. Whist, now!

Enter Molly.

MURPHY: Molly, darlin', is that you?

MOLLY: I am that.

MURPHY: I have news for ye.

MOLLY: They're sayin' that Terence O'Brian is here. (*Regarding Bunn*) Is that him? Well, it's the littlest man are often the great ones.

BUNN: I am not Mr. O'Brian. I am Professor Bunn, the distinguished oculist.

MURPHY: More than that, Molly, he's an eye-doctor! Molly, what would ye say if he were to tell me he could cure my blindness?

MOLLY: When he'd done it, I'd marry him tomorrow if he asked me. I can't say worse than that.

MURPHY: If he cured me, you'd marry him?

MOLLY: Yea, Pat—if he cured you.

BUNN: I feel convinced your cure will be effected in a few hours.

Exit Molly into Murphy's cabin.

MURPHY: I'll not be cured by you at all. It's some other way I'll find.

BUNN: My dear sir, a bargain's a bargain. I can't help the ladies running after me.

MURPHY: Maybe I can.

Enter Terence from park.

(*To Terence*) Terence, avick, it's the little Professor here I find is a traitor and a spy—and he'd beat be hanged, take my word for lt.

BUNN: Well of all the—if you'll kindly listen—

Molly appearing at door.

MOLLY: It's deeds more than words I'd listen to.

TERENCE: Yes. You shall have one chance of proving your usefulness. Deliver this letter to Lady Rosie's maid, up at the house. I have tried and failed. The sentries would not let me pass. Succeed, and your life shall be spared.

Bunn takes note as Sentry appears at gates. Bunn approaches him.

SENTRY: Passers-by will not pass by without a pass. If passers-by pass by without a pass, they will pass out and pass by. Them's my orders. Pass on.

BUNN: Listen, my good man. Everyone has his price. Now, if I walk on and come back again, what will you charge?

SENTRY: Bayonets! (*Does so*)

BUNN: H'm!

SENTRY: Passers-by will not pass by without a pass. If—

BUNN: Stop! I am going to show you a pass—several passes—which you've never seen before. Look at me. (*He mesmerizes the Sentry, puts him in a convenient attitude, then passes by him up avenue. The Sentry remains rigid*) Bong soir! (*Raises his hat, and exit*)

TERENCE: Mesmerism! I shall keep my eye on him—but he sha'n't keep his on me!

Enter Molly. She goes to well and draws some water.

MOLLY (*aside to Terence*): Listen, your honour. If ye stay here, bear me out in all I say before poor blind Pat, and say nothin' yourself of what ye see a poor girl doin' for the sake of—of friendship for a poor boy. (*As she goes across*) Are ye not afraid at all of having Carrig-Cleena for your hiding place?

(*She sits and begins to peel a bowl of potatoes which she has brought from cabin*)

TERENCE: Why should I be?

MOLLY: Don't ye know that it's haunted with fairies?

TERENCE: Well, I—

MOLLY: You don't believe in fairies? Few do nowadays under the Lord Lieutenant's rule, but Pat and me, we know they're true, don't we?

MURPHY: Yes, Molly.

MOLLY (*to Terence*): The Fairy Cleena is their queen. Sometimes she takes the shape of a peasant woman, and shows herself, they say. It's the Fairy Cleena herself has taken a fancy to Blind Murphy— she and her small folk do many little things for him—little enough, but helpful to a blind man that has no womenkind of his own. It's few evenings he'll not find his praties peeled for supper—by the small folk—and the water drawn—it's the fairies that do it. We know that now, don't we, Pat?

MURPHY: Yes, Molly, darlin'.

TERENCE: The Fairy Cleena?

MOLLY: Sure enough. We don't tell the other boys. They've left off believing in such things. It's only Pat and me that know the old tale's true, after all.

No 5. TRIO.—MOLLY, MURPHY, and TERENCE.
(Arthur Sullivan)

MOLLY: On the heights of Glantaun there's no voice that is human,
　　But sometimes, at night-fall, the lone passer-by
　　Will hear on the west wind the song of a Woman,
　　That calls him to follow the sound of her sigh.

MURPHY: It is Cleena who calls him—'tis Cleena the Fairy,
　　(Or so tells the old country legend, not I),
　　And if he be foolish or bold or unwary,
　　He'll follow the sound of her musical sigh!

MOLLY: And there in her Cavern of Dreams he'll lie dreaming,
　　A laugh on his lip while his life rushes by—

MURPHY: For the world where she dwells is the Fair World of Seeming,
　　The world that is found at the end of a sigh!

TERENCE: Yes, the world where she dwells is the Fair World of Seeming,
　　The world that is found at the end of a sigh!

ALL: The where she dwells is the Fair World of Seeming,
　　The world that is found at the end of a sigh!

Molly takes Murphy's hand and leads him; they exeunt.

TERENCE (*looking through park gates*): Rosie!

Enter Lady Rosie.

TERENCE: You had my note?

Enter Susan. She stands demurely waiting, with eyes fixed on ground.

ROSIE (*to Terence*): Yes. How do you do?—(*after glance at Susan*)—Darling!

TERENCE: I am quite well, thank you—(*after glance at Susan*)—dearest! And you?

ROSIE: Very well, indeed—(*aside*)—love!

SUSAN: Shall I wait, my lady?

ROSIE: Oh, are you there, Susan? No, you need not wait, Susan. Er— Susan

SUSAN: Yes, my lady?

ROSIE: Is that soldier a friend of yours?

SUSAN: The sentry, my lady? Well, my lady, I believe I do happen to have made his acquaintance.

ROSIE: You may talk to the sentry if you like.

SUSAN: Thank you, my lady.

ROSIE: You may even walk a little way with him, on his beat, up the coach road.

SUSAN: Thank you, my lady. (*She goes to Sentry. He is still rigid, in a mesmeric trance*)

TERENCE (*to Rosie*): I'm afraid the sentry is not quite himself—the fact is, my messenger who took my letter—

ROSIE: Oh, he had one for Papa, too.

TERENCE: For the Lord Lieutenant! A letter! From whom?

SUSAN (*to Rosie*): It's a curious thing, my lady, but he don't seem to take no notice.

ROSIE: It is his sense of discipline, Susan, because I am here. You can whisper to him that I shall not mind his walking up the coach road. I shall not report him for it.

SUSAN: Oh, I've told him you're dying for him to go, my lady. I'll tell him again. (*Goes to Sentry*)

TERENCE (*to Rosie*): You say my messenger had a letter for the Lord Lieutenant?

ROSIE: Susan said so—I have reason to believe she ia a painfully truthful girl.

TERENCE: What can it have been? (*Goes up*)

SUSAN (*to Rosie*): I can't upset his discipline not anyhow, my lady. But there's a gentleman coming down the drive who's winking at me, my lady. The one who brought the note—

ROSIE: Do you think you could—just for once—make the sentry—er, jealous! Do you think that would—er—move him?

SUSAN: I'll see what I can do, my lady.

Enter Bunn. He ogles Susan.

TERENCE: I must talk to this Mr. Bunn.

ROSIE: Don't interrupt them, please—to please me. (*She takes him up. Business with Susan*)

BUNN: Remarkably warm evening, miss—?

SUSAN (*coyly*): Susan.—Do you think so? I'm such a chilly mortal. Just feel my fingers! (*Offers hand*)

BUNN (*taking it*): Ah! cold hands, warm—

SUSAN (*coyly*): We are not alone. (*Indicating Sentry*)

BUNN: Oh, he won't take any notice.

SUSAN: I think perhaps he will, soon. I believe I saw him twitch.

BUNN: Oh, well, I don't want you to feel any restraint. I'll send him on his beat.

Susan turns up to Rosie and Bunn turns to Sentry and releases him from his mesmeric trance.

SUSAN (*to Rosie*): It'll be all right soon, my lady.

ROSIE: Thank you, Susan.

BUNN (*to Sentry*): Right!

The Sentry wakes. His expression changes as he sees Susan; he smiles. She goes to him.

SENTRY: Lord Lieutenant's domestics require no pass.

Exeunt Susan and Sentry arm in arm. Bunn is left astounded and disconsolate.

TERENCE: I want to talk to you, Mr. Bunn, on business. I hear you left a letter—

ROSIE: Oh, must you talk business now? I thought—(*Pouting*)

TERENCE: Well, the business shall wait. (*To Bunn*) But so must you. I am not going to let you out of my sight—

ROSIE: Need this gentleman wait? I thought—(*Pouts*)

Enter Susan.

TERENCE: Some one must keep an eye on him.

SUSAN: Could I help, my lady?

ROSIE: Susan! Why have you come back?

SUSAN: The sentry has just been made a prisoner by the Corporal, my lady—for talking to me.

ROSIE: But I thought the Corporal was a particular friend of yours?

SUSAN: That's just it, my lady, he is—most particular.

ROSIE: Then you had better go and talk to the Corporal.

SUSAN: Thank you, my lady. (*Exit*)

TERENCE: The problem is, how to take two persons from three persons, and not leave a remainder of one person.

ROSIE: I think I could do it with apples. Suppose you had three apples—

BUNN: Allow me. (*Produces three apples by a conjuring trick*)

No 6. Quartette.—Rosie, Susan, Terence, and Bunn.
(Arthur Sullivan)

Rosie: Two is company—three is none:
What's to be done?
From three take one—
One from three are two, I own
But that leaves one apple all alone!
Rosie, Terence, Bunn: Multiplication
Is vexation—
Division is as bad!
The rule of three
Doth puzzle me—
Subtraction drives me mad!
Terence: One remains, and if that be true,
What shall we do?
From three take two:
One from three will leave you one—
So two from three should leave us none!
Rosie, Terence, Bunn: Exhilaration!
Jubilation!
The problem fairly fought!
If one from three
Leaves one—(*that's me/he*),
Then two leaves nought—or ought!
They are surprised to find Bunn still left over. Susan has meanwhile re-entered.
Susan: I've discovered a useful fact
Certain to act,
You don't subtract!
Add one more to the three you've bought
And then divide—the remainder's nought!
All: Simple equation!
Calculation
The fruit of its labour bears!
Three apples glum
At once become
Contented happy pairs!

Dance.

Exeunt Terence and Rosie.

BUNN: So you are left in charge of me? Hadn't you better hold me
   tight, Susan? (*Business. They sit*)

SUSAN: It seems to me there's mysteries afloat. Who is this
   Mr. O'Brian?

BUNN: A very dangerous young man.

SUSAN: I love dangerous young men. Why have I to keep my eye on
   you?

BUNN: Why? Because I'm more dangerous than he is. He's jealous.
   You think I'm stout. I'm not. It's gunpowder.

SUSAN: Lawks! Why, you might go off!

BUNN (*aside*): So I might—if I can get the chance.
   Susan, you must take your eye off me for a few minutes. I'm going
   to change my costume.

SUSAN: What for?

BUNN: For the costume of the lean and slippered pantaloon, in my
   impersonations of the Seven Ages of Man. You do love dangerous
   men?

SUSAN: I've always had a leaning that way. That's why I lean to
   soldiers.

BUNN: Ah! I set my face against soldiers.

SUSAN: So have I, sometimes. But detectives is my craze. Here comes
   the Lord Lieutenant! You're not the Irish League?

BUNN: No. Scotland Yard!

SUSAN: A detective! That breaks my dream. (*Exit*)

Bunn enters Murphy's cottage, carrying costume, which he takes from carpet-bag.
Enter Lord Lieutenant, Countess, and Dr. Fiddle, and later, Rosie with
Terence at back. Rosie comes down innocently, and Terence exit hurriedly.

No 7. TRIO.—LORD LIEUTENANT, COUNTESS, and DR. FIDDLE.

(Arthur Sullivan)

LORD L.: I am the Lord Lieutenant, and
   It's well that you should understand
   I am the highest in the land—
      The Lord Lieutenant of Ireland.

COUNTESS: And I, his wife, of high degree,

Enhance my husband's dignitee!
FIDDLE: And I'm his private Chaplain who
    To some extent enhance it too.
ALL: For we three
        (I and he
    And the Reverend Dr. Fiddle, D.D.)
    Represent the dignitee
        And the serious side of Ireland!
            In Court dress,
                More or less,
    The country folk we try to impress
    With a proper sense of the seriousness
        Of the Lord Lieutenant of Ireland.

No 8. SONG—LORD LIEUTENANT with ROSIE, COUNTESS,
                and DR. FIDDLE.
            (Arthur Sullivan)

LORD L.: At an early stage of life
    I said I'll choose a wife,
    But where shall I find the particular girl
    Who is fit to be knit to a noble earl—
        Such a very particular
        Perpendicular
            Noble earl as I?
ALL: Such a very particular, etc.
LORD L.: I can't be too particular!
    Though few such girls there probably are,
    I intend to wait until I find
    A lady of that particular kind,
ALL: Such a very particular
        Perpendicular
{ROSIE, FIDDLE: Noble earl was he!
{COUNTESS: Noble girl was I!
{LORD L.: Noble girl she'll be!
LORD L.: Oh, that particular girl may share
        My very particular coronet!
    Who always moves with a stately air
        As though her life were a minuet!

Rosie, Countess, Fiddle: She always moves
    As though her life were a minuet!
Lord L.: So I waited years to find
  A lady to my mind,
  Till I came to the age of forty and three,
  When a certain particular girl found me—
    And that very particular
    Perpendicular
      Noble girl was she!
All: And that very particular, etc.
Lord L.: You can't be too particular
  At forty-three, whoe'er you are,
  So I set my teeth and shut my eyes
  And swallowed that matrimonial prize!
All: Such a very particular
    Perpendicular
{Rosie, Fiddle: Noble girl was she!
{Countess: Noble girl was I!
{Lord L.: Noble girl was she!
Lord L.: The sort of girl that you would not care
    To call "my darling," "love," or "pet"—
  But she walks through life with a stately air,
    As though her life were a minuet!
All: She walks through
    As though it all were a minuet!
Exit Rosie to rejoin Terence.
Lord L.: I may suppose, I think, that any one
  Who saw me standing thus would be deceived,
  And think I am a King!
Countess: No, not deceived.
  You are a King and I'm a Queen, my lord.
  The only difference that lies between
  Us and all other Kings and Queens is this—
  We are more dignified!
Lord L.: Much more. I am
  The only King, or representative
  Of Royalty (outside the characters
  Of Shakespeare's plays) who makes a special point
  Of talking in blank verse, and who insists

That every member of his family
And household shall converse in blank verse too!
Sir—Doctor Fiddle—

FIDDLE: Yes, your Excellency!

LORD L.: Go and enquire if one Professor Bunn
Has yet arrived: I am expecting him.
(*To Countess*) Professor he of elocution:
And with his elocutionary art
He mingles parlour magic. In a word,
He'll make a pudding in your hat—not mine—
Extract a rabbit from your pocket, or
An egg from your back hair.

COUNTESS: 'Tis false!

LORD L.: I mean
He could—not necessarily he will.
I have engaged him for our Infant Schools:
He'll interest the children. Send him here
At once.

FIDDLE: I'll put my best foot forward.

LORD L.: No,
Not forward—go out backwards, if you please.
Exit Fiddle.
I think it rather odd the peasantry
Do not assemble when we come and go
To cheer us.

COUNTESS: Yes. But let us cheer ourselves!
Can we not form a Royal group of two—
A family group in studied attitudes
Of dignity combined with perfect grace,
Such as a Royal Portrait Painter loves?
You standing there, the left leg well advanced
To show the calf: your elbow resting on
A marble pillar (*we'll imagine that,
Also a curtain and a thunder-cloud Behind*) That's exquisite! (*Stands
contemplating him*)

Terence and Rosie enter at back.

ROSIE (*aside*): Go! Fly to your hiding place—to Carrig-Cleena!

TERENCE: To-morrow—you will meet me to-morrow?

ROSIE: Yes! (*They kiss. Exit Terence*)

COUNTESS (*to Lord Lieutenant*): I by your side,
 Holding your hand and gazing at you thus—(*Kneeling*)
ROSIE (*coming down*): What are you doing?
COUNTESS: Showing all the world
 That Kings need not depend upon their crowns
 For dignity. Some monarchs have, I know,
 In English history—who when dethroned
 Forgot their pride; but we should not!
LORD L.: Not we!

No 9. SONG.—COUNTESS.
(Edward German)

When Alfred's friends their King forsook
 His pride did he forsake!
  'Twas in the year eight-seven-eight,
  That Alfred who is called "The Great"
Forgot his pride, and undertook
 To cook the oatmeal cake!
A thing, it cannot be denied,
A King should not have ever tried!
I profit by my History Book,
And oatmeal cakes I never cook,
Because I know that it would look
 Undignified to bake!

Dame History I now invoke
 Of Second Charles to tell!
  King Charles, in sixteen-fifty-one,
  His Parliamentary foes to shun,
Climbed up a gnarled and knobbly oak
 In shady Boscobel!
A thing, it cannot be denied,
A King should feel undignified!
So I have never climbed an oak
(A task beyond some Royal folk),
And also, if the branches broke,
 Undignified as well!
Exit Rosie. Dr. Fiddle advances.

FIDDLE: Your Majesty!

LORD L.: Glide, Dr. Fiddle, glide!
    Pray do not skip! Toes more turned out, and eyes
    Turned up, to show the whites; the body bent:
    Humility combined with grace—that's it.
    Remember that position, sir, and mine!

FIDDLE: The elocutionist, Professor Bunn,
    Has not arrived yet; but some stranger left
    This note for you. (*Hands note*)

Enter Molly and Murphy at back.

LORD L. (*glancing at it*): Anonymous! Ah, well,
    In these days men who cannot sign their names
    Can make their mark!

(*reads*) "The Lord Lieutenant's warned that the rebel Terence O'Brian
    is in the neighbourhood—his secret meeting place is Carrig-
    Cleena. The writer has been force against his will into joining the
    rebel society, and will be much obliged by the Lord Lieutenant
    exterminating same at as early date as possible."

MOLLY (*aside*): What's that?

LORD L.: Pooh!

COUNTESS: Fudge!

FIDDLE: Bosh!

LORD L.: Dr. Fiddle, you
    Forget yourself! This letter is not bosh;
    Go, send a messenger for extra troops,
    And we'll exterminate these rebels: point
    Your toes.

Exit Dr. Fiddle, Lord Lieutenant and Countess critically watching him.

MOLLY (*to Murphy*): There's been a double-faced traitor somewhere.
    Do ye hear, Pat?

MURPHY: I do, Molly. I wish it was in my heart to tell ye that I can
    see as well!

MOLLY: If ye could, would I be holdin' your hand?

MURPHY: That's it. Ye would not.

LORD L.: What have we here?

COUNTESS: From his appearance I
    Should say an impecunious performer
    Upon the violin.

MURPHY: Not at all, your honour. It's a poor fiddler I am.

COUNTESS: Bow, when the Lord Lieutenant speaks.

LORD L.: Bow thus. (*Showing him*)

Are you in need of alms?

MOLLY: No, eyes, you honour, seein' he's blind.

LORD L.: "Alms" with an "l"—Bow!—were the alms I meant.

MOLLY: Arms with an el-bow were the arms I meant. Come, Pat, it's
not the Lord Lieutenant I want to be splittin straws with.

LORD L.: Kiss hands when you retire.

Murphy kisses his hand to the Countess.

COUNTESS: He kissed his hand
To me.

MOLLY: He's blind, ma'am. He wouldn't have done it else. Come, Pat.
I'll show ye to your door.

LORD L.: Stay—an idea!

COUNTESS: That make a two to-day!

LORD L. (*to Murphy*): Do you perform upon the bagpipes, knave?

MURPHY: Do I? Molly, darlin', fly into my cabin like the angel without
with wings that ye are, and bring the pipes. His Lordship will not
ask of me twice when he's heard me once.

He hands fiddle to Molly, who exits into cottage.

LORD L.: I ask because I fancy it would lend
(*If possible*) additional effect
And dignity to my appearance, if
My comings and my goings were announced
By bagpipes, played a little in advance
Of where I walk.

COUNTESS: It might attract a crowd.

LORD L.: It might. So, if I pay a pound a week
To this poor man to pipe in front of me
Whenever I leave home till I return,
I shall, I think, successfully combine
Cheap charity with much advertisement—
The soul of up-to-date philanthropy;
Charity which, though it begin at home,
Is seen and heard for miles.

COUNTESS: An excellent idea!

MURPHY: It is that! A pound a week! It's an offer of marriage I see
peepin' out o' that offer as soon as I get my eyesight, which I'll find
somehow by this time to-morrow, if I go blind in the search.

Enter Molly with pipes.

MURPHY: I'm at your service and in it, Lord Lieutenant, darlin', from this moment.

MOLLY (*aside*): You! Is it you that has turned the traitor? Oh, I wouldn't have believed it! (*Turns slowly and exit*)

MURPHY: But ye do, mighty quick! Ah, Molly, if ye knew everything, ye would understand more.

COUNTESS: Come, now, prepare to pipe.

ROSIE (*entering*): Papa! Papa!
 Oh! is it true the soldiers have been summoned
 To make a raid on Carrig-Cleena, and
 To catch and hang the rebels?

LORD L.: Yes, my chuck!
 They will parade at sunset, here. And I
 Shall then address them, as I love to do,
 A few soul-stirring words.

COUNTESS: And so shall I.

LORD L. (*to Murphy*): Prepare to pipe some proud appropriate air
 Indicative of victory.

MURPHY: Molly, Molly, you've filled my heart with emptiness!

Murphy begins to play a doleful air.

LORD L.: I have no ear for music, but is that
 Indicative of victory? It sounds to me
 Like groans and moans—

MURPHY: It's the groans and moans of the vanquished that ye hear, your honour: how can ye have a victory without a defeat at all?

Exit playing, being led by Chaplain and followed by Lord Lieutenant and Countess.

ROSIE: At sunset! How can I warn him? Oh, what shall I do?

No 10. SONG.—ROSIE.
(Edward German)

 O setting sun,
 You bid the world good-bye!
 Your course is nearly run,
 And soon the day will die!
 Night, with gentle sigh,
 Will spread her pall!

Hope was my sun,
        That crossed a summer sky!
My day is nearly done,
        The night already nigh:
        Love's a laugh—a sigh—
                And that is all.

        Not so,
My doubting heart!
        Although
The sun depart
And leave the earth in sorrow;
        Despair
        Is but to-night.
        Is there
        To be no light
Upon the morrow?
Not so, my doubting heart!

Enter Terence.

TERENCE: Dearest!

ROSIE: You have not gone?

TERENCE: I tried to, but I've been hanging about here—

ROSIE: You will be, dear, if you don't take care! Papa has been warned; the soldiers are going to raid Carrig-Cleena—you have been betrayed.

Enter Susan.

TERENCE: That's Professor Bunn! Where is he? I knew he was dangerous! (*Runs up*)

SUSAN: Ah!

ROSIE (*to Susan*): Where is he, Susan?

SUSAN: Oh, he's safe enough, my lady.

TERENCE: Not he!

Rosie and Terence exeunt. Enter Bunn, disguised as a very old man, from cabin.

SUSAN: You don't know him as I do! He's a nero.

BUNN (*coming down*): Not a Nero, Susan. I cannot marry a lady without aspirations.

SUSAN: Co away, you silly old man!

BUNN: Susan! (*Taking off his beard*)

Terence and Rosie enter at back.

SUSAN: Mystery on mystery!

TERENCE: So you are trying to escape in disguise?
(*Presenting pistol*)
ROSIE: Don't let it go off, please! (*Both girls stop their ears*)
BUNN: You are frightening the ladies, air. (*Goes to them, and shields himself between them*)
MOLLY (*entering, followed by girls*): Listen, Terence O'Brian! Do ye know the soldiers are out—and a traitor somewhere?
TERENCE: Yes, and I know where he is! There!
MOLLY: Wait, lest ye shoot an innocent man. It is in my mind to say it is another—though it is not in my heart to say who. But the game's not up—it is only beginning.
TERENCE: How?
MOLLY: This way. I have thought how to keep Carrig-Cleena clear of the soldiers. They are mostly men from Devonshire, and they say such are mighty afraid of fairies. We'll tell them the tales of the place bein' haunted. We'll tell them how the Fairy Cleena catches all the good-lookin' boys and keeps them sleepin' and dreamin' for fifty years.
TERENCE: They won't believe everything you choose to tell them. They're ordinary soldiers, not the Intelligence Department.
MOLLY: They shall believe it. It's myself that's goin' to appear to them as the Fairy Cleena herself—and seein' is believin'.
TERENCE: There really might be something in it!
BUNN: Now, perhaps, you will let me tell you why I put on this costume. Not for any purposes of escape. Not from any selfish motive. I am prepared, for the purpose of hoaxing the soldiers, to impersonate a gentleman who has been kept a prisoner by the Fairy—er—
TERENCE: Cleena?
BUNN: Precisely—by the Fairy—er—er—for fifty years. That is why I have adopted this costume. It is the nearest thing to Rip Van Winkle I had by me.
ROSIE: How clever!
BUNN: Yes, I am pretty quick at getting at an idea. If you will all follow my instructions, I have no doubt I shall be able to frighten these soldiers into fits.
TERENCE: Mr. Bunn, I am sorry—I was hasty.
BUNN: Well, you were a little free with the shooting-gallery. But there' I don't bear malice. Say no more about it.
TERENCE: Thank you. You are very kind.
SUSAN: A nero, if ever there was one! And like a nero to deny it!

No. 11. Quintette.—Rosie, Molly, Susan, Terence, and Bunn.
(Arthur Sullivan)

Bunn: Their courage high
    You may defy
    For by and by
    By means of my
    Behaviour sly
    You'll find that I
    Shall terrify
    The soldiery,
    And make them shy
    Of going nigh
  The caves of Carrig-Cleena.
All: If you and I
    Ourselves ally,
    And by and by
    Together try
    To mystify
    The soldiery,
    I don't see why
    They shouldn't fly
    And mutiny
    And rather die
  Than go to Carrig-Cleena!

  If all of us care to dare retell
  A similar wary fairy tale,
  They'll turn a military tail
    On the caves of Carrig-Cleena!
Principals exeunt. Enter Soldiers to Girls.

No. 12. Entrance and Chorus Of Soldiers, with Girls.
(Arthur Sullivan)

Men: That we're soldiers no doubt you will guess
    From our marchin' to fifin' and drummin',
  As well as the form of our dress,

Which we fancy is rather becomin'.
By lookin' again you will see
  That our regiment's number eleven;
From that you will gather, maybe,
  That we come from the County of Devon.
GIRLS: Come the Saxon raiders!
   And when they come,
   Shall we be dumb?
  Hark, ye red invaders—
It's not us ye'll drown with fife and drum!
MEN: We should be, if in Devonshire now,
  (As it may be amusin' to mention)
All cow-'erds who're attendin' a cow,
  Instead of brave men at attention!
But, work bein' over, maybe,
  As it now is a quarter to seven,
Sir Roger de Coverley we
  Would be merrily dancin' with someone in Devon!

ENSEMBLE.

MEN: That we're soldiers, no doubt, you will guess, etc.
GIRLS: Come the Saxon raiders, etc.
MEN: From Devon, happy Devon, have we come,
GIRLS: From Devon, Saxon Devon, have ye come,
MEN: A-marchin' to the rattle of the drum.
GIRLS: To drown us with the rattle of a drum.
Enter Sergeant.

No 13. SONG—SERGEANT and CHORUS.
(Edward German)

SERGEANT: Now this is the song of the Devonshire men
CHORUS: With a bimble and a bumble and the best of 'em!
SERGEANT: And the maids they have left on the moor and the fen—
CHORUS: With a bimble and a bumble and the best of 'em'!
SERGEANT: There was Mary Hooper, and Mary Cooper, and Jane
 Tucker, and Emily Snugg, and Susan Wickens, and Hepzibah
 Lugg, and Pretty Polly Potter, and the rest of 'em!

CHORUS: And Susan Wickens, and Hepzibah Lugg, etc.

SERGEANT: The Sergeant he came a-recruiting one day!

CHORUS: With a bimble and a bumble for the best of 'em:

SERGEANT: And the maids cried alack! when the men went away—

CHORUS: With a bimble and a bumble for the best of 'em!

SERGEANT: There was Thomas Perry, and Thomas Merry, and Jan Hadley, and Timothy Mudd, and Harry Budgen, and Oliver Rudd, and Ebenezer Pincher, and the rest of 'em!

CHORUS: And Harry Budgen, and Oliver Rudd, etc.

SERGEANT: So the men marched away in their bright scarlet coats,

CHORUS: With a bimble and a bumble and the best of 'em!

SERGEANT: Though they shouted "Hooray" they had lumps in their throats,

CHORUS: With a bimble and a bumble and the best of 'em!

SERGEANT: And the maids fell a-crying, as maids often do, Saying, "Oh, will our lovers be faithful and true?" But some day they will march into Devon and then, All the maids will be taking the names of the men— There'll be Mary Perry, and Mary Merry, and Jane Hadley, and Emily Mudd, and Susan Budgen, and Hepzibah Rudd, and pretty Polly Pincher and the rest of 'em!

CHORUS: There'll be Susan Budgen, and Hepzibah Rudd, etc.

SERGEANT: The Sergeant he may come recruiting once more,

CHORUS: With a bimble and bumble and the best of 'em

SERGEANT: There will always be Devonshire men for the war.

CHORUS: With a bimble and a bumble and the best of 'em!

SERGEANT: There'll be young Tom Perry, and young Tom Merry, and young Jan Hadley, and little Tim Mudd, and young Hal Budgen, and Juvenile Rudd, and a little Ebenezer, and the rest of 'em!

CHORUS: There'll be young Tom Perry, etc.

Enter Terence.

TERENCE (*to Sergeant*): And so, my honest fellow, you don't forget the girls you have left behind you?

SERGEANT: No, zur. There be Mary Hooper and Mary Cooper and Jane Tucker and Emily Snugg and Susan Wickens and HepzibahLugg and pretty Polly Potter—(*sighs*)

TERENCE: And yet—and yet—you are all going to Carrig-Cleena!

SERGEANT: Ess. There be Thomas Perry and Thomas Merry and Jan
    Hadley and Timothy Mudd and Harry Budgen and Oliver Rudd
    and myself and—
TERENCE: Poor fellows!
SERGEANT: Eh?
TERENCE: Suppose—merely suppose—that when you reach the caves
    of Carrig-Cleena, which as you know, are haunted by fairies—
    (*repeating with emphasis*) which, as you know, are haunted by fairies—
SERGEANT: Aw! I an't ayerd nort about that!
TERENCE: Haven't you? You will before long. What's this?
Enter Susan, hurriedly, over bridge.
SUSAN: Oh, my mistress, Lady Rosie,
    Daughter of the Lord Lieutenant,
    Has been greatly agitated
    By a very strange encounter!
Rosie enters.
KATHLEEN: What's the matter, noble lady?
    Calm yourself, and try to tell us.
(*Music (by Edward German) commences*)
ROSIE: It is past my comprehension!
    On the road from Carrig-Cleena
    Suddenly a man addressed me—
    Quite a harmless aged person,
    Who, in answer to my question,
    Told me he was then escaping
    From the caves of Carrig-Cleena,
    From the Fairy Cleena's clutches!
    What he meant I cannot tell you—
    This is he who now approaches!
Bunn enters, somewhat in the manner of Rip Van Winkle.
ALL: This is he who now approaches
    From the caves of Carrig-Cleena,
    From the Fairy Cleena's clutches!
KATHLEEN: Speak, aged man,
        And say what troubles ail you!
    As quickly as you can—
        Before your senses fail you!
ALL: Speak!
Bunn singles out the Sergeant and addresses him.

No. 14. Song.—Bunn and Chorus.
(Arthur Sullivan)

Bunn: Many years ago I strode
    Down the Carrig-Cleena road;
    Night coming on, tired out, I lay
    Where the legend says the fairies play!
    But the tales I had heard of fairy tricks
        Were never believed by me;
    Then I was a youth of twenty-six,
        But now I'm eighty-three!
All: Now he's eighty-three!
Bunn: Round and round the fairy ring,
    There I heard the fairies sing;
    This is the fairy song I heard,
    Do I remember it?—every word.
        Da Luan, da mort, da Luan, da mort
        Angus da Dardine!

    Many, many people may
    Disbelieve what I do say—
    Once I was young and foolish, too,
    And an ignoramus, just like you;
    But whenever you hear of fairy tricks,
        Don't laugh at 'em any more.
    Then I was a youth of twenty-six,
        But now I'm ninety-four!
All: Now he's ninety four!
Bunn: Dancing round the fairy ring
    All that time I've had to sing;
    Though you may not believe a word,
    This is exactly what occurred,
        Da Luan, da mort, da Luan, da mort
        Angus da Dardine!
Molly (*heard off*): Da Luan, da mort, da Luan, da mort
        Angus da Dardine!
Chorus: Ah!
Bunn: Hark! 'tis she' Beware! Take care!
Molly (*off*): "Come away.

Come away," sighs the fairy voice,

"Come to the caves of Carrig-Cleena!

For there I make all aching hearts rejoice—

Come, come away"

ALL: 'Tis Cleena! The Fairy Cleena!

MOLLY: Yes! 'tis I!

ALL: 'Tis Cleena!

Molly enters and stands on bridge. She carries a flowering branch in her hand, and wears a wreath of wild flowers.

MOLLY: For my voice may lie

In the west wind's sigh,

Like the wailing note of the Banshee's cry,

Saying, "Come, come, come away,

To the caves of Carrig-Cleena!"

{ROSIE: Come!

{SOLDIERS: Ah!

{MOLLY and GIRLS: Da Luan, da mort, da Luan, da mort

Angus da Dardine!

The Soldiers are greatly affected—others pretend to be.

Enter Murphy from park.

MURPHY: Is that Molly's voice I hear—Molly O'Grady's?

NORA (*aside*): Hush! It's frightening the soldiers we are!

ROSIE: It is the Fairy Cleena!

TERENCE: The Queen of the Fairies!

MURPHY: Is it the Queen of the Fairies ye are?

MOLLY: I am that! I have taken Molly's shape and her voice for my appearance.

MURPHY: It's a wise choice ye made, Cleena, darlin'. It's her voice I'd follow whenever it called—even to the caves, on a dark night.

BUNN: Fool! Look at me, and tremble!

MURPHY: I'd be a fool to tremble with lookin' at anyone, bein' blind. Cleena, darlin', ye may not know it, but it's a miraculous cure for my blindness that I'm lookin' for. It's my mind was made up to come to your caves this very night to ask for it as a gift from the fairies. I'll follow you.

MOLLY: No; the fairies cannot cure you of your blindness. You will be disappointed, Blind Murphy.

MURPHY: Not at all. It's certain sure I am that I'll be able to see by the mornin'—

MOLLY: Be warned—do not trust too much in the fairies, poor Blind
Murphy. (*Exit*)

TERENCE: You will be kept in the Cavern of Dreams for fifty
years!

MURPHY: Bedad, then, I'll be after puttin' a few things in a bundle for
my visit. (*Exit into cottage*)

SERGEANT: Now, diddee iver see sich a chubble-headed vule's 'er is in
awl yer born days? I niver didden!

No. 15. FINALE.
(Arthur Sullivan)

BUNN: Their fathers fought at Ramillies,
　　And they're prepared to scatter all
　　　The armies in the world's arena;
　　But they owe it to their families
　　　To shun the supernatteral—
　　　　They don't intend to go to Carrig-Cleena.

MEN: No, we don't intend to go to Carrig-Cleena!

BUNN: They'll be shot at break of day
　　For refusing to obey!

MEN: We don't intend to go to Carrig-Cleena!

Bunn goes up with Sergeant.

ENSEMBLE.

TERENCE (*to Rosie*)
Sweetheart, betake
　Thyself to bed;
Lie not awake
　With aching heart or head;
And for my sake
　Be not consumed with dread,
For I'll be safe at
　Carrig-Cleena!

ROSIE (*to Terence*)
Be, for my sake,
　By prudence led;
Keep wide awake,
　To-night go not to bed;
For I shall quake
　Till you have wisely fled
The neighbourhood of
　Carrig-Cleena.

GIRLS (*to Soldiers*)
For goodness' sake
　The danger dread;

SOLDIERS.
For glory's sake
　Though we have bled,

Let nothing shake
    What you have wisely said.
His warning take—
    By his advice be led,
And do not go to
    Carrig-Cleena.

And never quake
    Before a shower of lead,
No power shall make
    Us go, as we have said—
We will not go to
    Carrig-Cleena.

Enter Susan.

RECITATIVE.

SUSAN: Your ladyship?
ROSIE: Well?
SUSAN: Your Papa approaches!
ROSIE (*to Terence*): Farewell!
TERENCE: Farewell! Parting is such sweet sorrow—
SUSAN: Pray, pray, sir, say goodbye until to-morrow.
TERENCE: Farewell!
ROSIE: Farewell!
TERENCE: Farewell!
SUSAN: Oh, pray be careful! (*Exit Terence*)
ROSIE: Ah, I indeed am full of care!
SERGEANT (*to Soldiers*): Attention!
Enter Lord Lieutenant, Countess and Fiddle.
LORD L.: Soldiers, the time has come for your
    departure
    Upon a most important expedition,
    Namely, the capture of a noted rebel,
    Whose hiding place we think is Carrig-Cleena.
    Before you leave upon your dangerous errand,
    Her ladyship and I will both address you
    A few well-chosen words of stirring nature,
    Which will, I have no doubt, affect you deeply!
COUNTESS: Soldiers, prepare,
    To leave your bivouacs;
On comfortable glare
    Of campfire turn your backs.
Near is the hour
    Appointed for parade—
      Soldiers, I bid you take heart!

LORD L.: Sound the trumpet, roll the drums,
Prepare to do or die!
Dulce et decorum est
Pro patria mori!
Wheresoe'er the foeman comes
Be there to bar the way!
North, or South, East, or West,
Britons stand at bay!

COUNTESS: Vive la guerre!
Who'll think of crying "Pax"?
The favours of the fair
A hero never lacks.
In Beauty's bower
Shall Mars hang up his blade—
Soldiers, prepare to depart!

LORD L.: Only bravest of the brave
Deserve the fairest fair;
Shall the French monopolize
The shout of "Vive la guerre"?
Shall a Briton be a slave
To any foreign foe?
While the flag of Britain flies
Britons answer "No!"

ALL: Shall a Briton be a slave
To any foreign foe?

GIRLS: While the flag of Britain flies
Britons answer "No!"

SOLDIERS (*murmuring*): We don't intend to go to
Carrig-Cleena.

COUNTESS: A shout from all and each
Should follow such a speech!

FIDDLE: But none is heard.

COUNTESS: Enthusiastic cheers
Should fall upon our ears!

LORD L.: But none occurred.

SOLDIERS: We don't intend to go to Carrig-Cleena.

LORD L.: The bugle's joyful note
May prove an antidote
To such a scene! (*Bugle sounds*)

FIDDLE: They do not move at all
    In answer to its call—
THREE: What does it mean?
SOLDIERS: We don't intend to go to Carrig-Cleena!
LORD L., COUNTESS, FIDDLE: Now how is this, and what is this?
      Their manner's most mysterious;
    And why is this, and what's amiss?
      I trust it's nothing serious!
    I thought I heard them say,
      In a disrespectful way,
    That they don't intend to go to Carrig-Cleena!
ALL: No! We/they don't intend to go to Carrig-Cleena.
ROSIE: O papa!
        Though, Papa,
      Their courage is undaunted,
    Could you make them face a place
      By Fairy Cleena haunted?
        She will keep
        Them fast asleep
    Till they're a mass of wrinkles,
  Old and bent, with great long beards as white as snow!
CHORUS: Though their hearts are all undaunted,
      Naught could make them face a place
      By Fairy Cleena haunted?
LORD L., COUNTESS, FIDDLE: Hush, my child!
        Blush, my child,
      A lady of position
    Should not lend an ear, my dear,
      To vulgar superstition;
  Such things do not happen, as you ought to know!
CHORUS: Such a thing has happened, as we'll quickly show!
Sergeant leads Bunn forward.
BUNN (*to Lord Lieutenant*): Many, many years ago,
      Just how many I don't know,
      I was an ignoramus too,
      For I laughed at fairies just like you!
      But as I fell under fairy tricks
        It's lucky I'm still alive;

> For I was bewitched at twenty-six,
> > And now I'm a hundred-and-five.

CHORUS: Now he's a hundred and five!

BUNN: Round and round the fairy ring,
> > All that time I had to sing;
> > Though you mayn't believe a word,
> > That is exactly what occurred

BUNN and SOPRANOS: Da Luan, da mort, da Luan, da mort
> > Angus da Dardine!

CONTRALTOS and MEN: Ah!

FIDDLE: I do not think this doddering old dotard
> Believes what he has told us!

COUNTESS: Dr. Fiddle!
> I do not think that anyone in Ireland
> Would dare to try to hoax the Lord Lieutenant!

LORD L.: I think that even dotards would not dodder
> To that extent!

Molly's voice heard off.

MOLLY: Come away

ROSIE: Hark! Hark!

CHORUS: Hush! Hush!

MOLLY: Come to the caves of Carrig-Cleena!

ROSIE: "Come away," sighs the Fairy Voice,
> > "Come to the caves of Carrig-Cleena!
> For there I make all aching hearts rejoice,
> > Come, come away!"

GIRLS: "Come away," sighs the Fairy Voice,
> "Come away! Come away!"

MEN: Come away from the haunted caves of Carrig-Cleena!

ALL: "Come away," sighs the Fairy Voice, etc.

The Soldiers disperse, panic stricken. The Lord Lieutenant, Countess, and Fiddle are awed, and exeunt; the Girls pretend to be and exeunt. When the stage is empty, Murphy comes from his cabin, and is crossing the bridge as the curtain falls.

END OF ACT I

Act II

SCENE.—*The scene represents the exterior of the Caves of Carrig-Cleena; a romantic spot in the mountains. It is moonlight. Peasant men with Dan discovered. One of them, Mickie, is acting as Sentry, on the look-out.*

No. 16. OPENING CHORUS.
(Arthur Sullivan)

MEN: Is there anyone approachin'?
    Is the coast quite clear?
  Walkin', runnin', ridin', coachin',
    Is there anybody near?
    Is there anything to fear?
  Is there anybody poachin'
    On the privacy of our preserves?
      We're getting nervous!
DAN: No! No one comes,
    The coast is clear;
  But distant drums
    I faintly hear.
MEN: Though the summer night is dumb in
    My attentive ear,
  And there's nobody a-comin'
    To disturb us, never fear,
    Yet I fancy I can hear
  Now and then a distant drummin',
    And it gets upon my high-strung nerves—
      The Saints preserve us!
MICKIE: Halt there!
DAN: What do you see, Mickie?
MICKIE: Somebody that's keepin' invisible!
All Men retire into caves out of sight.
DAN (*to Mickie*): Stay where ye are, sentry. It's an honourable post ye
    are holdin', mind that.
MICKIE: Holdin' the post, am I? Didn't ye tie me to it yourself with
    your own two hand' and one of my braces? Bedad, it's the post
    that's holdin' me, not me the post at all

TERENCE (*Heard off*): Erin-go-bragh!

DAN: Maybe it's only Terence, after all.

TERENCE (*entering*): It is. Where are the boys?

DAN: They thought you was the soldiers.

TERENCE: I see. Have they gone far?

DAN: Not far, considerin' the start they had.

Men re-enter.

TERENCE: Well, you need think no more of the red-coats.

DAN: It's little enough we think of them. We treat them with contempt.

TERENCE: They have refused to come here, and we are perfectly safe.

ALL: Hooroo!

TERENCE: Professor Bunn, our new recruit, succeeded in persuading them that this place is haunted by fairies. They are frightened to death of coming here.

DAN: And it's the little Professor did that?

TERENCE: He was mainly responsible for the details of the plan.

DAN: Then it's a credit to Ireland he is. What do ye say, boys?

No. 17. CHORUS.
(Edward German)

Bedad, it's for him that we'll always employ
A name that St. Patrick himself would enjoy;
For St. Patrick himself was a broth of a boy—
    And liked to be called it in Ireland!

MICKIE: Halt there!

TERENCE: What is it?

MICKIE: The swatest enemy ye ever saw. It's Kathleen, the darlin', and the other colleens.

Enter Kathleen, followed by girls.

No. 18. JIG.
(Edward German)

CHORUS: Ah! Ah! Ah!
    In St. Patrick was a broth of a boy!
    For St. Patrick was a broth of a boy!
    For St. Patrick was a broth of a boy!

TERENCE: I am sorry you are out of breath, for I gather that you have brought news of importance. Am I right? I f you cannot speak, nod your heads.

All the Girls nod vehemently. Enter Molly.

MOLLY: Ye are all goin' to be killed.

TERENCE: Dear me! That is calculated to take one's breath away. Can you tell me any more?

Molly shakes her head.

NORA: Where's my Mickie?

MICKIE: Here I am, Nora dear, stickin' to my post like a blessed martyr to his stake.

NORA: For what are ye statin' up there alone to be shot at?

MICKIE: I'm bound to stay, darlin', and that's the truth. My runnin' away would mean my undoin'.

Nora releases him.

MOLLY: You are surrounded. The Lord Lieutenant and the soldiers are coming here.

TERENCE: But the soldiers said they were afraid to come.

KATHLEEN: They changed their minds.

DAN: That's like the soldiers—the cowards! And it's my belief the little Professor was deceivin' you all the time, and not the soldiers. It's a traitor and a spy he is.

TERENCE: It is possible.

DAN: What do ye say, boys?

No. 18a. CHORUS.
(Edward German)

Och! the spalpeen! Let him drown!
Hang him! Bang him! Knock him down!
Thrash him! Bash him! Crack his crown!
    He's a traitor to Old Ireland!

DAN: Whisht now—what's that?

Bagpipe heard in distance.

TERENCE: Is it a pig in pain? (*Goes up*)

MOLLY: Not at all. It's Blind Murphy with his music.

KATHLEEN: It's Blind Murphy has taken service with the Lord Lieutenant.

DAN: What's that?

NORA: The truth.

DAN: Then it's comin' here as a spy he is.

MOLLY: Not at all. He thinks he can get cured by the fairies—he said so.

DAN: A spy would say anything.

CHORUS (*commence*): Och, the spalpeen! etc.

MOLLY: Stop your foolishness!

DAN: It's while the stable door's still open I'll not wait here to be taken like a horse in a trap.

NORA: It's surrounded your trap is—ye can't get out of it by leavin' it.

DAN: Then it's the Book of Fate that's written dead against us. What do ye say?

MOLLY: Say? That if the Book of Fate is written against us, it's the Book of Fate want re-writin', and it's the old Irish character we'll use in doin' it. For Dame Fortune, the old schoolmistress, may put an Irish boy in a corner, but it's his back he'll put to the wall in spite of her. Eh, Terence?

TERENCE: Yes; Black Care will never ride a winner in the Irish race, while I'm in it.

No. 19. SONG AND CHORUS.—TERENCE.
(Arthur Sullivan)

Oh, have you met
A man in debt
And almost out at elbows?
Who all the while
Can show a style
As grand as any swell beau's?
Who loves a horse,
And though, of course,
He'll choose the best to ride on,
Will hunt the fox
On any crocks
That he can get astride on!
Whose life's a race at breakneck pace,
With Care dropped well behind him,
If you've not met that portrait yet,
It's Ireland where you'll find him!

CHORUS: Whose life's a race at breakneck pace, etc.

TERENCE: Who's not afraid
    Of man or maid,
  And thinks fair play a jewel,
    Who'll kiss your wife,
    But give his life
  To miss you in the duel!
    Who borrows what
    He hasn't got
  To lend a poorer brother,
    And when he pays
    You, never says
  He used it for another!
  Who's always near a laugh or tear,
    Just as you may remind him,
  If you've not met that portrait yet,
    It's Ireland where you'll find him!
CHORUS: Who's always near a laugh or tear, etc.
TERENCE: Who's learnt each vice,
    From drink to dice,
  That's known from here to Hanley,
    But all the time
    Commits no crime
  That's called ungentlemanly!
    So we'll forgive
    The way you live,
  Though some may call it shady;
    You'd sooner die
    Than tell a lie,
  Except to save a lady!
  True chip of block, old fighting stock
    Who never looked behind 'em!
  If you've not met good soldiers yet
    It's Ireland where you'll find 'em!
CHORUS: True chip of block, old fighting stock, etc.
DAN: Good for you, Terence, avick. It's to you that we'll trust to get
  us out of our distress, and not to any mesmerisin', ventriloquizin',
  advertisin' quack of a cockney character impersonator. It's
  surrounded with spies we are, and he's one of 'em, and Blind
  Murphy's another—and what's this if it's not two more?

Enter Rosie and Susan.

ROSIE: Terence! (*She throws herself into his arms*)

DAN: The Lord Lieutenant's own daughter! How's that for spyin'?

MOLLY (*to Dan*): It's the gentleman's sweetheart she is.

DAN: What's that?

TERENCE: Yes; I did not tell you before; this lady and I are engaged.

ROSIE: Not quite engaged, dearest. You are engaged to me, but I
    cannot be engaged to you without Papa's consent, and that we shall
    never have. We are lovers indeed—but engaged, alas, no!

SUSAN: Handkerchief, my lady? (*Handing it*)

ROSIE: Thank you, Susan. (*Drying her eyes*)

DAN: And is it you, Terence O'Brian, rebel and patriot, that are
    contemplatin' unholy matrimony with one of those Saxon serpents
    that trample our country under their heels? It's a double-faced
    traitor ye are. What do ye say, boys?

CHORUS: Och, the spalpeen! etc.

DAN (*to Terence*): And smilin', too! It's a handful of slugs shall fly in
    your smilin' face! (*Getting blunderbuss*)

ROSIE (*to Terence*): Don't let them throw slugs at us, dear, will you?
    Not even snails. I couldn't bear it.

TERENCE: No, darling, don't be afraid.

SUSAN: Salts, my lady?

TERENCE (*as Dan advances with blunderbuss*): My friends, perhaps I
    owe you an explanation. This lady and I met in London before we
    understood the incongruities of our positions. We fell in love, and
    have never yet succeeded in falling out. You will not blame us when
    you hear the peculiar circumstances of our first meeting.

No. 20. DUET—TERENCE and ROSIE WITH CHORUS
(Arthur Sullivan)

TERENCE: 'Twas in Hyde Park beside the Row
        That she and I first met;
    Against the rails I pressed my suit
        (Although the paint was wet);
CHORUS: Ah me! The paint was wet,
TERENCE: I said "Love me, and I'll love you,"
        She could not answer "No!"
    For she was one and I was two,

That day in Rotten Row.

CHORUS: Oh, she was one and he was two, etc.

ROSIE: 'Twas at a ball, the lights were low,
    And he and I had met;
  He told me of that hopeless suit—
    I felt my eyes grow wet;

CHORUS: She felt her eyes grow wet;

ROSIE: He whispered, "How can I win you?"
    I answered "I don't know,
  For I was won when you were too
    That day in Rotten Row."

CHORUS: For she was won when he was too, etc.

TERENCE: Now do you still think a man a traitor for being faithful to the lady he loves?

MOLLY: Is it you, Black Dan, will say that with Kathleen there hangin' on you arm and every word ye speak!

ROSIE: What a nice girl! Have you a lover?

MOLLY: No, ma'am.

SUSAN: Poor thing! (*A whistle is heard*)

BUNN (*off*): Erin-go-bragh!

TERENCE: The password.

DAN: Then it's either the Professor or Blind Murphy—one of the two—and spies both. Whichever it is shall have a warm welcome. What will we do?

CHORUS (*commence*): Och, the spalpeen! etc.

MOLLY: No! Get out of sight and hearin', while I see which it is.

All exeunt silently. Enter Bunn cautiously. He is dressed as on his first entrance, Act I.

BUNN: Is this the place? Erin-go-bragh! Erin-go-bragh! No; there's no one here. No one at all.

MOLLY (*coming down*): Ye're not Pat, but the Professor—the Saints be praised!

BUNN: Eh? Erin-go-bragh, my dear. Erin-go-bragh a thousand times. (*Shaking her hand warmly*) Are you so glad to see me?

MOLLY: I am that. I was afraid it might be—someone else.

BUNN: Afraid it might be? (*Ogling her*) Are we alone?

Enter Susan.

MOLLY: You've a sweetheart here?

BUNN: I can see that. (*Looking at Molly*)

MOLLY: Then it's a double-faced lover ye must be, seein' she's behind you.

BUNN (*turning*): Susan! (*Greeting her effusively*)

SUSAN (*aside*): My detective! Are you going to arrest them all and carry them off by force?

BUNN: Not by force. I employ stratagem with any number of criminals over ten. (*To Molly*) Where are the—er—b-hoys?

MOLLY: They are preparin' a warm welcome for ye.

BUNN: Really? I didn't know I was so popular.

Enter Chorus.

CHORUS (*they seize Bunn*): Och, the spalpeen! Let him drown! etc.

At the end his coat is torn up his back, etc.

Enter Terence and Rosie.

BUNN: I really did not know I was such a favourite. You've nearly torn me in pieces. Really, I'm a perfect scarecrow.

TERENCE: Listen, boys, and you, Mr. Bunn. Lady Rosie has kindly given me an idea. It's as a scarecrow you were employed by me; you undertook to scare the soldiers—and failed. You shall have one more chance. We are surrounded and are going to be attacked by a regiment of English infantry, eight hundred strong. If you succeed in frightening them away, your life shall be spared by us. If you fail—

BUNN: Yes, if I fail—it is not likely—but if I fail—?

TERENCE: As one of us you will, of course, suffer death at their hands.

BUNN: Leave everything to me, sir.

TERENCE: Everything is left to you—except a way of escape. What do you propose?

ROSIE: Might he not have a minute for reflection?

BUNN: Reflection? Now you've given me an idea. Have you ever heard of Professor Bunn's apparitions?

ROSIE: No.

BUNN (*surprised*): Dear me, how large the world is! Where is the young person who appeared as the Fairy Cleena last evening?

MOLLY: I'm here.

BUNN: This time I will improve your appearance. I will make you appear weird—terrible—unearthly.

MOLLY: I'm mighty obliged to you.

BUNN: Listen! Every passer-by that sets foot in this place you will address in terms of passionate affection, and invite him to stay with you for fifty years.

MOLLY: I will not.

BUNN: Eh?

MOLLY: What would I do that for?

BUNN: To frighten him away. The Fairy Cleena is supposed to do it.

MOLLY: That's her affair; there's nothin' I'd do it for.

BUNN: Why on earth not?

No. 21. CONCERTED NUMBER.—ROSIE, MOLLY,
KATHLEEN, DAN, BUNN, and CHORUS.
(Edward German)

MOLLY: I cannot play at love,
    But when I love,
  Gladly I'll say I love,
    For then I'll love.
  But if I love not you,
  How shall I say I do?
    Love then would be a lie,
  And Love is true.

KATHLEEN: Some maids have played at love
    Who've not a love;
  But where's the maid in love
    Who's got a love;
  Who'll think "I love's" a thing
  Lightly to say or sing
    To every passer-by
  That's listening?

BUNN: Did you ever? Well, I never!
    No, I never, never did!
  Pretty Molly, Miss O'Grady,
    I'm uncharitably chid,
  I'm suggesting nothing shady,
  For the feelings of a lady
    I have the deepest sympathy, of course.

ROSIE (to Bunn): Vulgar varlet, doesn't scarlet
    Your unhappy face suffuse?
  In the presence of a lady
    Kindly mind your P's and Q's;
  Though a humble peasant maidie

She has the feelings of a lady,
   Your conduct is unpardonably coarse.

ENSEMBLE.

DAN.	MEN.
Hearken minion! Her opinion	Listen, stupid! hasn't
Cupid Is identically mine:	Even taken you in hand?
She's a modest little maidie,	That the feelings of a lady
And her feeling's very fine.	You can so misunderstand?
In a humble peasant maidie	Don't you think a peasant maidie
The refinement of a lady—	Has the feelings of a lady?
A feeling that I thoroughly	I hope that you are bitten by
endorse.	remorse.

ROSIE, KATHLEEN, MOLLY, GIRLS: But if I love not you, etc.

ALL: Some maids have played at love, etc.

Exeunt all except Bunn and Susan.

SUSAN: It strikes me there's mysteries on mystery's head. How is it that you, a detective and a nero, let yourself be put upon?

BUNN: Ah! that's where I'm clever; that's where I'm cunning. Don't you see, it's part of the game?

SUSAN: It seems to me the game's hockey, with you for the ball and everyone else with a stick.

BUNN: I daresay it does look a little like that, at first.

SUSAN: It looks more like it every minute.

BUNN: Susan, will you endeavour to recollect that there are such things as wolves in sheep's clothing—and that I am one of them? Will you kindly remember that this is an age of shame, and that, as any Irishman will tell you, the English rose by climbing over the shamrock?

No. 22. SONG.—BUNN, with SUSAN.
(Edward German)

Oh, the age in which we're living strikes a man of any sense
As an age of make-believe and imitation and pretence:
And it's gradually growing more impossible to see
The difference between what people are and seem to be!
Our ladies grow more youthful now, the longer they're alive,

And reduce their ages annually, after thirty-five;
But for such miscalculations they will always make amends
By liberally adding to the ages of their friends,
BOTH: By liberally adding to the ages of their friends.
BUNN: And if Aesop wrote his fables
       In the present year of grace,
    He perhaps would turn the tables
       On the tortoise in the race:
For which goes quicker on ahead, and stays the faster there,
The imitation tortoise-shell or imitation hair?

There's the vulgar imitation of a true philanthropist
Who sends a hundred thousand—to be published in a list—
Which purchases a title (*as he possibly intends*),
With an imitation coat of arms, and imitation friends.
Then his wife—a charming lady with an imitation blush—
Will hold a big reception, where Society will rush
To see her imitation of a Duchess, in the style
Of her imitation welcomes with an imitation smile!
BOTH: Of her imitation welcomes with an imitation smile!
BUNN: But a bona fide Duchess
      Will endeavour to forget
    The aggravating clutches
      Of eternal etiquette
  By assisting at an imitation charity bazaar
As an imitation barmaid in an imitation bar!

Now the passage to a Drawing-Room's a matter for alarms,
When the elbows of the Dowagers mean passages of arms,
For ladies (*not of slim age*) love to push and fight and scratch,
To imitate a scrimmage in a Rugby football match!
But if noble women do forget they're noble, now and then,
There are plenty of young ladies who behave as gentlemen—
There's the tailor-maid, who imitates the cheeriest of chaps,
  (And owes a pretty figure to her tailor too, perhaps,)
BOTH: And owes a pretty figure to her tailor too, perhaps,
BUNN: While silly servant maidies
      Dress in imitation silk,
    And think they look like ladies

When they're taking in the milk—
But though they take the milk in, that's the only thing they do,
And the milk takes them in sometimes, being imitation too!
(*The following verse does not appear in the vocal score*)
Though an age of imitation, let us hope the time is near
When an imitation Army will entirely disappear!
For John Bull has a cupboard, and it isn't wise of John
To keep inside that cupboard nothing but a skeleton.
Though imitation patriots persistently pooh-pooh
The progress of their country, and her little Empire too,
And bolster fact with fiction, and are satisfied, forsooth,
That they are not taradiddlers—only editors of truth!
"It would be so inexpensive,
And reduce the income-tax,
If, when others grew offensive,
Little England spouted 'Pax'!
For we shouldn't need a Navy, nor expensive Army Corps"—
If only we could count on having imitation wars!

Enter Terence and Rosie, and afterwards Chorus.

TERENCE: Mr. Bunn, Lady Rosie has another idea for you. As there is a
difficulty about the fairy appearance, why not try to alarm the soldiers
by letting them see a weird and grotesque figure skipping about the
mountain in the moonlight? Why not impersonate a goblin?

BUNN: Well, sir—why not? I daresay you would do it very nicely.

ROSIE (*to Bunn*): Oh, of course I meant you to do it.

BUNN: Me? My dear lady—have you ever seen a goblin?

ROSIE: No, never—have you?

BUNN: No; but I have seen their pictures. The generally accepted idea
of a goblin is something ugly—small and mean-looking.

ROSIE: Yes, I know.

BUNN: A mixture of the insignificant and the grotesque.

ROSIE: Yes, I know.

BUNN: Well, there you are, you see—I really can't make myself plainer.

ROSIE: No; I know. I didn't think you'd want to.

TERENCE (*men entering*): You see, unless you do something—and we
can think of nothing else—I know I shall not be able to restrain
the temper of this meeting—they will summon Judge Lynch in a
moment.

Dan and Men and Girls have entered.

DAN: It's arrived he is now, your honour. (*With blunderbuss*)

SUSAN (*aside to Bunn*): Hasn't the time come yet to arrest them?

BUNN: Patience. (*To Dan*) Wait—I will make one more attempt to—to save your lives. If this young lady will assist me, I will impersonate a goblin, running after a fairy. It won't be quite like the old-fashioned idea of a goblin. I dare say it will look more like a scene out of "Romeo and Juliet." But it is all I can do for you. I will make myself as frightful as I can.

No. 23. CONCERTED NUMBER AND DANCE.
(Arthur Sullivan)

KATHLEEN: Sing a rhyme
    Of "Once upon a time,"
  When nothing went contrairy!

TERENCE: When goblins all lived underground,
  In spite of all the gold they found,
  Because a fairy always frowned
    If a goblin met a fairy.

ALL: Sing a rhyme
    Of "Once upon a time",
  The goblin and the fairy.
    Sing a rhyme
    Of "Once upon a time,"
  When nothing went contrairy!

BUNN: I'm a goblin grim and glary—

SUSAN: I'm a little feminine fairy—

BUNN: Hobblin' goblin!

SUSAN: Airy fairy!
  Fairy Queen and Goblin King.

BUNN: With a leap and a creep and a cat-like spring,
    The fairies' match is the Goblin King.

SUSAN: Fairy catches a glimpse of you,
    She runs one way, you run too.

BUNN: Hobblin' goblin!

SUSAN: Wary fairy!

BUNN: Little contrary—

SUSAN: Wise and wary—

BUNN: Lighter than airy—

SUSAN: Innocent fairy—
      Fairy Queen and Goblin King
They exeunt, dancing, and re-enter for second verse of duet.
CHORUS: Tune your lay,
      Tune your lay.
ROSIE: Tune your lay
      To quite another day
      When maids are mercenary.
TERENCE: And goblins bring the gold they've found
   To tempt the fairies underground—
   And that's the reason, I'll be bound,
      One seldom sees a fairy.
ALL: Tune your lay
      To quite another day,
      A goblin and a fairy.
      Tune your lay
      To quite another day
      When maids are mercenary.
BUNN: I'm a monster Millionairy—
SUSAN: I'm a little Vanity Fairy—
BUNN: Goldfish (*oldfish*),
SUSAN: Angle, dangle,
      Fairy Queen and Golden King.
BUNN: Oh, I am the catch of the London spring,
      The greatest match is the Golden King.
SUSAN: Fairy catches a glimpse of you,
      You run one way, she runs too.
BUNN: Hobblin' goblin,
SUSAN: Wary fairy,
BUNN: Hanover Squary,
SUSAN: Happy Pairy,
BUNN: Millionairy,
SUSAN: Vanity Fairy,
      Fairy Queen and Goblin King.
CHORUS: Sing a rhyme
      Of "Once upon a time",
      The goblin and the fairy.
General dance and exit. All exeunt except Bunn, Rosie, and Terence. Molly enters.

MOLLY: There's someone coming this way now. But it's not frightened he seems.

TERENCE: If you cannot arrange to frighten anyone, Mr. Bunn—

BUNN: It shall be done, sir—it shall be done. (*To Molly*) Have you any objection to making the appearance I mentioned, without delivering the passionate love-address?

MOLLY: I have not.

BUNN: Then kindly step into that cave.

MOLLY (*aside*): It's Blind Murphy that's comin'—he'll not notice my appearance.

Exit Molly into cave R.

BUNN (*to Rosie*): Excuse me, miss—do you sing?

ROSIE: Oh, yes!

BUNN: Love songs?

ROSIE: Oh, yes!

BUNN: Do you know any love song of a cheerful nature, one that implies that the singer has a sweetheart from whom she never means to separate—in fact a love song without the phrase "good-bye," or "farewell," or "we must part" occurring in it?

ROSIE: Oh, no! there are none published.

BUNN: I thought not.

TERENCE: You forget the set of verses, darling, that I wrote for you on your birthday. They are not published, but—

ROSIE: But they are a gentleman's love song.

TERENCE: They were intended to represent the lady's feelings as well. I see no objection to your singing them to me.

BUNN: Then will you kindly step behind that rock and begin singing them when I sneeze twice? Your voice will appear to come from the apparition. I will arrange my apparatus. (*Exit into cave*)

ROSIE: If you think it right, darling, I do. Everything you ever think right, I will always think right.

TERENCE: That's how I always like you to think, darling. That's why I know we shall be happy together.

Enter Bunn.

BUNN: I have arranged the apparatus in the cave. Kindly step behind this rock.

ROSIE: We are quite ready.

Exeunt behind rock by side of cave R. Enter MURPHY.

BUNN: Oh! it's Blind Murphy, the impostor, is it?

MURPHY: It is that—at present. But it's not blind I'll be any more when I've pretended I've spoken with the fairies. That's why I'm here. Have the boys all gone?

BUNN: Yes; they heard your—er—music—and thought it might be coming nearer. Listen. Did you really believe it was the Fairy Cleena that appeared in Molly's shape last evening?

MURPHY: I did not. I saw through that. But I believe in tellin' Molly I've come here and had a talk with the real Cleena and got my sight back from her. It'll be the miraculous cure I'm lookin' for.

BUNN: Look there! (*Pointing to cave on right. Molly's reflection appears*)

MURPHY: Saints preserve us!

BUNN: Can you see through that? Do you notice it's transparent?

MURPHY (*awed*): It's Molly's shape, but it's not flesh and blood this time. Is that you, Cleena, ma'am? Speak, Cleena, and say you're not yourself at all, but only Molly as ye were the last time—speak, for the love of—

BUNN: Speak, lady—speak! (*Sneezes*)

ROSIE (*from behind rock*): Do you wish me to speak or sing, Mr. Bunn?

MURPHY: It's not her voice. It was Molly's shape and Molly's voice before—but this is only her shadow, and not her voice at all. It's the real Cleena this time, sure enough, that I never believed in, the Saints forgive me!

BUNN: Sing, lady, sing, as thou wouldst only sing to one thou lovest; and tell me this—am I the one thou lovest?

ROSIE: How dare you say that, Mr. Bunn?

BUNN (*to Murphy*): You see it's not me she loves, so it's you.

MURPHY: Divil a doubt—I'm the happy man, bad luck to it! What will I do?

BUNN: Listen—and then run and warn the soldiers and the Lord Lieutenant, and tell 'em to keep away—a good long way. (*Sneezes and exit*)

No. 24. SCENE.—LADY ROSIE with MURPHY and TERENCE.
(Edward German)

ROSIE: Listen! Hearken, my lover, hearken to my voice,
Hearken and rejoice,
I love thee! I love thee!

MURPHY: I have no choice—she loves me.

ROSIE: Nought shall divide

And tear our souls asunder!
Nor land, nor tide,
   Nor hail, nor rain, nor thunder!
I love thee!
My arms enfold thee,
My love shall hold thee,
   For ever and for ever!

{   MURPHY (*in despair*): Her charms will hold me for ever!
{   TERENCE (*embracing Rosie*): My love shall hold thee for ever!

Murphy falls senseless. The lighting now changes to sunrise.
Enter Bunn, Molly, Kathleen, Nora, Dan, Girls, and Men.

BUNN (*to Terence*): I fancy I've frightened someone this time, sir.

NORA: Who is it?

KATHLEEN: It's Blind Murphy.

MOLLY: Oh, it's frightened to death he's been! (*Kneeling by him*)

ROSIE: Oh, and I helped to do it!

TERENCE: No, no; he has only fainted.

BUNN: A success at last, sir, eh?

TERENCE: No, Mr. Bunn—a failure. The idea was that he should run off and tell the soldiers, and frighten them away; and instead of that he has fallen in a faint. Another failure, Mr. Bunn, and I think the last one.

BUNN: Oh, never say die, sir!

TERENCE: No, I'll leave it to the Lord Lieutenant to say that.

BUNN: We'll have one more trial, sir.

TERENCE: Yes, and we will all be tried together. Listen, Mr. Bunn, if you try to save your own skin by playing a double game, I shall put a bullet through your brain, or at any rate through your head. I think it is perhaps a kindness to let you know this.

BUNN: Thank you, sir. You've quite taken a fancy to me!

(*Exit into cave*)

Murphy shows signs of regaining consciousness.

MOLLY: Did the lady frighten you with her singing, Pat?

MURPHY: Molly! Is it really you, Molly?

MOLLY: Who else would it be?

MURPHY: I thought I saw—

MOLLY: If ye thought ye saw anything, it's dreaming ye must have been, bein' blind, poor boy.

MURPHY: Yes, bein' blind.

TERENCE (*to Murphy*): You are accused of having come here as a spy.

DAN: It's hangin' is too good for him, but it's all we have to offer. (*Preparing a rope*)

TERENCE: He must be tried first and sentenced afterwards.

DAN: The other way's safest with spies. But have it your own way.

TERENCE: Who will stand as the prisoner's friend?

DAN: It's no friend he has among us, to stand or lie for him.

MOLLY: That's where ye're wrong. It's a strange thing that the only man among ye should be a girl! I'll stand as his friend, your honour—it's what I'd do for anyone.

TERENCE: You can question the prisoner. The cross-questions will come after.

MOLLY: It's not cross mine will be at all. I'm just doing this out of kindness—ye understand that, your honour?

TERENCE: Yes, I understand. Go on.

MOLLY (*to Murphy*): Now, Blind Murphy, ye are charged with bein' a traitor. Are ye a traitor?

MURPHY: I am not.

MOLLY: That's every bit good enough for me. (*To Terence*) Will ye be wantin' to hear any more evidence, your honour?

TERENCE: Yes; he is accused of writing an anonymous letter to the Lord Lieutenant warning him of our society.

MOLLY: The Lord Lieutenant we overheard readin' an anonymous letter—did ye write it?

MURPHY: I never put my name to such a document in my life.

MOLLY (*triumphantly*): Hear that now!

TERENCE: He is accused of coming here as a spy.

MOLLY: A spy! (*To Murphy*) How could ye be spyin' if ye were blind? Tell me that.

MURPHY: I could not.

ROSIE: There's some sense in that.

MOLLY: There's no sense in it, ye mane. A blind man can't be a spy—that's proved—and it's one more question will close the case. Haven't ye been blind since ye were a gossoon that little? Speak, Pat dear—ye've only got to say it on your oath, and the case is concluded. It's the easiest thing in life; askin' the question at all is like puttin' a frill on a ham-bone—it's not a necessity, but makes a finish. Come now, haven't ye been blind since ye were a gossoon?

MURPHY: No, I've never been blind at all. It's a lyin' thief that I've been—I've never been blind. I never had the heart to tell ye, seein' that ye pitied me—and pity's near akin to love, they say—though it's a mighty poor relation. I've never been blind—I wish I had before I saw ye look like that, Molly!

MOLLY: Ye've never been blind—and me holdin' your hand, and peelin' your praties—and pretendin' it was the fairies!

DAN: Wouldn't such be a spy?

TERENCE: Yes. (*To Molly*) Have you anything more to say?

MOLLY: Yes—no.

ROSIE: He has spoken the truth now.

MOLLY: They say that will shame the divil. I know it has shamed me.

TERENCE: He is banished. (*To Murphy*) You have been able to see all these people when they didn't know it—if they know it, you shall never see them again.

Exeunt all, leaving Molly and Murphy. Before her exit Rosie goes to Molly and quietly kisses her.

MURPHY (*to Molly*): Have you stayed to say good-bye, Molly?

MOLLY: It's not sure I am that I have.

MURPHY: Then it's only the cold stones of my native town that I'll be sayin' it to.

No. 25. SONG.—MURPHY.
(Edward German)

Good-bye, my native town—
Wrapped in your summer gown,
No tears are running down
    Your pretty face,
You cannot feel nor hear,
Why should you shed a tear?
How can you know how dear
    I hold this place?
It's only you and I
That have to say good-bye;
Ah! won't you heave one sigh
    When I depart?
Why do you look so gay?
Won't you pretend to say
"Pat, if ye go away,

I'll break my heart"?
Good-bye, my native place—
Almost a human face,
Almost a woman's grace
    You have for me.
You know there's never been
One word of love between
Me and a real colleen—
    There'll never be.
Good-bye! Good-bye! Good-bye!
(*Music continues under the following brief dialogue*)
MURPHY: Won't ye be sayin' good-bye, Molly?
MOLLY: No, Pat.
MURPHY: It's only a little word.
MOLLY: Yet it's a mighty big lump it makes in me throat wid stickin'
    there. I'll not say good-bye, Pat, because—
MURPHY: Yes, dear?
MOLLY: Because—

No. 26. DUET.—MOLLY and MURPHY.
(Edward German)

MOLLY: I love you! I love you!
    What joy can compare
With all the sweet madness
    That lovers may share?
For an ocean of sadness
    A world of despair,
Are lost in "I love you,
    I love you, my darlin', I do!

Ah! where is the world, dear,
    The world that we knew,
The old world, the cold world,
    Before I met you?
We've done with the old world,
    We're off to the new—
Because, dear, I love you,
    I love you, my darlin', I do!

Our love is our new world,
    A world of our own,
Where I may be queen, dear,
    Because we're alone;
Though our home may be mean, dear,
    I'll sit on a throne,
Because I love you!

BOTH: I love you! I love you!
    What joy can compare, etc.

Exeunt. Sergeant Pincher enters stealthily, as if searching for someone concealed. Kathleen, Nora, and Girls enter to him. Other soldiers follow the Sergeant. Terence enters.

KATHLEEN (*to Sergeant*): Are ye lookin' for anything—or anybody?

SERG: Ess—rebels. (*Regarding Terence and Girls*) Be you a gatherin' o' rebels?

TERENCE: No, we are a-gathering of mushrooms. Sir, you will no doubt think me very stupid, but what are you waiting here for? And hadn't you better go away?

SERG: Well, of awl the chubble-'eaded vules! We be under orders to wait for the Lord Lieutenant.

TERENCE: Poor fellows! And at any moment the Fairy Cleena, who haunts this spot, may catch sight of you, and keep you here for fifty years. What will Mary Hooper and Mary Cooper and Jane Tucker and the rest of them think then?

SERGEANT: There be Mary Hooper and Mary Cooper and Jane Tucker and Emily Snugg and Susan Wickens—

TERENCE: I know—I know. But where will they be in fifty years? What will become of them—and of you?

SERGEANT: Aw! I an't a-short nort about that!

TERENCE: Poor fellows! Pawns in the game of government. Playthings of unprincipled politicians! Poor deluded, patient, wooden soldiers!

SERGEANT: Eh?

TERENCE: Listen. I wouldn't dishearten you for worlds, but—listen!

No. 27. SONG.—TERENCE, with CHORUS.
(Arthur Sullivan)

There was once a little soldier
    Who was made of wood:

He always did his duty,
    And he proudly stood
Very stiffly at attention
    As a soldier should—
        Rat-a-plan! Rat-a-plan!
He was always very ready
    To receive hard knocks,
He and all his wooden brothers
    In the same big box:
Where their master chose to put them
    They would stand like rocks—
        Rat-a-plan! Rat-a-plan!
He did his duty just like a man!
But kindly remember, if you can,
    He was but a wooden soldier!
CHORUS: Rat-a-plan! Rat-a-plan! etc.
TERENCE: Now that little wooden soldier
    (As we all must do)
Grew gradually older
    Than he was when new,
Till at last I grieve to tell you
    That he broke in two—
        Rat-a-plan! Rat-a-plan!
But it really did not matter,
    For his price was cheap;
And as broken wooden soldiers
    Are no good to keep,
He was thrown with other rubbish
    On a rubbish heap—
        Rat-a-plan! Rat-a-plan!
"You do your work as long as you can—
But nobody wants a broken man,"
    Said the brave little wooden soldier!
CHORUS: Rat-a-plan! Rat-a-plan! etc.
Exit Terence, with Kathleen and girls.
SERGEANT: Now diddee iver zee sich a chubble-'eaded vule's er is in
    awl—
Enter Lord Lieutenant and Countess. The Soldiers range themselves in rank.
LORD L.: There are no rebels here—as I expected.

Here truly's military expedition
That sets out after rebels and arrives
Before them. We are first upon the field.

COUNTESS: Looking back
At English history, I do not know
Of any Queen who, on the eve of battle,
Kissed every single soldier in the ranks!

LORD L.: I think we should have heard of such a thing.

COUNTESS: We should; for 'twould have been a graceful act.
And our posterity shall hear of it—
From me.

Enter Bunn, unnoticed.

COUNTESS: Sergeant, come here, and I will kiss you first.

He comes down reluctantly, Bunn by his side, hidden from Countess and Lord Lieutenant. The Soldiers gradually exeunt by the closing step.

BUNN (*to Sergeant*): Do what I tell you, and you sha'n't be kissed.

As Countess and Lord Lieutenant go aside, Sergeant bends down and Bunn whispers to him.

LORD L. (*to Countess*): I may presume, I think,
That you intend to kiss the soldiers on
Their foreheads?

COUNTESS: Certainly; the kind of kiss
You give the debutantes at Drawing Rooms.

LORD L.: Such are too often only blank salutes
Of powder—which goes off when I discharge
That canon of my duty.

COUNTESS (*to Sergeant*): Can you bend
Gracefully, like a willow, from the waist?
I cannot reach your brow unless you do.

Bunn, standing behind Sergeant, nudges him.

SERGEANT: I be a turmit hawer,
    From Debbenshire I came;
    My parents be 'ard-working vokes
        An' I be just the zame.
            An' tha vly, ha, ha!
            Tha vly, ha, ha!
        Tha vly be on tha turmits,
            An' tez awl my eye vur me tu try
        To keep min off tha turmits.

LORD L.: He's either hard of hearing or insane!
  He thinks that we asked him to recite
  Some poem of his childhood.
COUNTESS (*to Sergeant, speaking a little louder*): Can you bend?
  I cannot kiss your forehead as you are.
SERGEANT: 'Twas on a Vriday morning,
        Avore the break of day,
      That I tuked up my turmit haw
        An' tridged dree miles away.
LORD L.: No, no, my man, to-morrow you shall join
  My Elocution Classes, but to-night
  The Countess wishes—
SERGEANT: I zune did get a place ov wark,
        I tuked it by the job;
      An' ef I 'ad my time again
        I'd zunder go to quad.
          An' tha vly, ha, ha!
          Tha vly, ha, ha!
        Tha vly be on tha turmits,
          An' tez awl my eye vur me tu try
        To keep min off tha turmits.
BUNN (*appearing to Lord Lieutenant*): Good morning! The Lord
  Lieutenant, I think?
LORD L.: Are you a rebel?
BUNN: No, my lord, no! I am—amongst other things—a member of
  the Society for Psychological Research. I've come here in search of
  fairies—and, by Jingo, sir, I've found 'em; the place is full of 'em.
SERGEANT: There's zome delights in haymaking,
        And a few delights in mawing,
      But ov all tha trades that I like best,
        Gie me tha turmit hawing.
BUNN: It's easy enough to see what's the matter with this poor man—
  he's bewitched. It's not safe to stay here, that's very certain. If I
  were you, my lord, I should get home to bed.
LORD L.: Sir, you amaze me!
BUNN: Ah! (*Pleased*)
LORD L.: I see at length
  My Chaplain is approaching; he is stout
  Though staunch, and lagged behind; he'll prove to you

That fairies can't exist. Come, Dr. Fiddle.

Enter Fiddle. He is panting.

LORD L.: Endeavour to remember that you are
 A learned Doctor of Divinity,
 And not a grampus.
 I want you, if you please, or if you don't,
 To preach your sermon to this gentleman,
 Who thinks this place is haunted. I perceive
 That to your faults of literary style
 The Countess has already shut her eyes—
 As I will do, I promise you. Begin.

Lord Lieutenant sits and prepares to slumber.

FIDDLE (*taking bulky packet from pocket and addressing Bunn*):
 This sermon I intended for to-morrow,
 In which I deal with vulgar superstitions
 So rife among the peasantry of Ireland.
 This sermon providentially I carry
 In my tail pocket—it is somewhat bulky,
 For I have made it thoroughly exhaustive—
 In fact, it is a question which will be, sir,
 The most exhausted when the sermon's ended—
 Myself, my subject, or my congregation.
 The subject I divide into ten headings,
 Each heading into twenty sub-divisions,
 Bristling with arguments and long statistics,
 Which prove entirely to my satisfaction,
 And will, I think, to yours, when you have heard
  them,
 That there are not, have never been, and cannot
 At any future time be in existence
 Such things as Fairies, Pixies, Nymphs, or
  Brownies,
 Hobgoblins, Gnomes, or other apparitions.

BUNN (*having made several unavailing attempts to interrupt and escape
 from the Chaplain, who has buttonholed him*): Your Excellency, I am
 quite satisfied—

LORD L.: That fairies don't exist? I'm glad of that;
 And I myself am also satisfied
 There are no rebels here.

COUNTESS: I do not think
    That anyone in Ireland—
LORD L.: Would rebel
    Against the Lord Lieutenant. So I think (*producing the*
    anonymous letter)
    The man who wrote this letter telling me
    Of rebels is the first, the very first
    And only man who ever tried to hoax
    The Lord Lieutenant. He shall be the last!
    A thousand guineas is the sum I offer
    For his discovery, or information
    That leads to it!
BUNN (*taking letter*): Permit me. I am Professor Bunn, the eminent
    expert in handwriting. Ah! I thought so! I can tell you who wrote
    this. I wrote it myself. A thousand guineas I think you said?
    (*Chuckles*)
LORD L.: I never break my word; and you shall have
    The thousand guineas.
BUNN: Thank you, my lord. I knew I could trust the word of a
    nobleman.
LORD L.: I never break my word; and I have said
    That I will shoot all rebels that I catch.
    You, in this letter, prove that you are one.
BUNN: Against my will, my lord!
LORD L. (*to Sergeant*): Let him be shot at once; if that be not
    Enough, let him be shot at twice, or thrice—
BUNN: My lord—
LORD L.: Summon the firing party!
BUNN: Whether 'tis nobler in the mind to suffer
    The slings and arrows of outrageous fortune,
    Or to take arms against a sea of troubles,
    And by opposing end them!
He is carried off by Sergeant. Enter Molly and Murphy.
MOLLY: Listen, Lord Lieutenant! It's banished my Pat has been for
    bein' a traitor to the rebels. And it's us that's goin' to show them
    we wouldn't betray them for the world. Come out of your hiding,
    boys!
Men and girls begin to enter.
MOLLY: Now, Pat, spake the truth and shame your accusers!!

MURPHY: Is it me that ever wrote a letter to ye in my life, Lord
    Lieutenant? Me that cannot write at all?

MOLLY: Why didn't ye say that before?

MURPHY: It's not a thing worth mentioning. (*To Lord Lieutenant*) It's
    not your friend I am at all! I'm the reddest rebel here.

CHORUS (*to Murphy*): Hooroo! Whirroo!

Soldiers enter.

LORD L.: Arrest these men, and let them be shot at once—if that be
    not enough—

Soldiers prepare their muskets. Enter Terence.

TERENCE: Stop! I am the leader of these men! If any one is shot—

LORD L.: Let him be shot at once; if that be not—

*Terence stands out. Susan runs across and throws herself into his arms,
between him and the Soldiers.*

SUSAN: No! My mistress would wish this done if she was here—(*Enter
    Rosie*)

ROSIE: I am. Thank you, Susan.

SUSAN: Shall I stay here, my lady?

ROSIE: No, thank you, Susan. (*Takes her place in Terence's arms*)

LORD L. (*to Rosie*): Who is this gentleman? Though you forget
    Yourself, can you inform me who he is?

COUNTESS: A common rebel.

ROSIE: Nay, a Commoner,
    Whom love has crowned my King.

COUNTESS: Tush!

LORD L.: Listen, girl!
    Apart from being daughter of a Viceroy,
    Remember you're of ten times royal birth;
    For, as is generally now the case
    Among the English aristocracy,
    Some of the richest if not the bluest blood
    Of all America flows in your veins.
    Your ancestors (*upon the other side*)
    Comprise two Railway Kings, a Copper Queen,
    And half-a-dozen Pork-pie Potentates.
    The democratic principles that must
    Lie in your blood with such an ancestry
    Will prompt you, I am sure, to love a Lord,
    And no one else. Release my daughter, sir.

Rosie: Papa, this gentleman is—(*to Terence*) Tell Papa
    who and what you are.

Terence: I'm descended from Brian Boru.

Peasants: Hooroo!

Terence: My blood is the elegant hue—

Peasants: True Blue!

Terence: That flows in the veins of the fortunate few
        Who are sons of the Kings of Erin!

Lord L.: I did not know that your descent was royal.
    That fact removes the first objection which
    I have to you as a husband for my daughter.
    But one objection still remains; 'tis one
    Which is, I fear, quite insurmountable.
    I cannot let my daughter marry one
    Who has been shot for treason—as you will
    Be shot in half an hour. I think that you
    Will understand that this is impossible.

Terence: Yes. If in company with these rebels I am to suffer a felon's
    death in half an hour, I cannot expect you to trust your daughter's
    happiness to me. I quite see that. There is nothing more to be said.
    It is a perfectly reasonable objection.

Bunn has been brought on.

Bunn: Pardon me. There is this to be said. It has just struck me. (*To
    Lord L.*) If we had guessed (*as we ought to have guessed*) that you,
    being a scion of a noble English house, had so much American
    blood in your composition, we should not have rebelled against
    you. America is the friend of Ireland. You are an English
    nobleman. Therefore you are nowadays more than half American.
    Therefore you are our friend. How do you do? I am glad we met.
    We are no longer rebels. It would be absurd to shoot us.

Lord L.: That sounds conclusive—

Bunn: It is conclusive. What do you say, b-hoys?

No. 28. Finale.
(Arthur Sullivan and Edward German)

With a big shillelagh, though somebody may accidentally
    knock ye down,
With a frightful whack on the dignified back of your typical

Saxon crown,
It's yourself that'll take, for your dignity's sake, little
notice of that at all!
If you'll not forget it's the strict etiquette of a typical
Irish ball!
Ah!
For St. Patrick was a broth of a boy!
For St. Patrick was a broth of a boy!
For St. Patrick was a broth of a boy!

General dance
Curtain

A Note About the Author

Basil Hood (1864–1917), Arthur Sullivan (1842–1900) and Edward German (1862–1936) were famous British composers and lyricists. Both German and Sullivan wrote and played music at an early age. Hood's career began in the British Army, where he wrote plays as a hobby. They created the bulk of their work during the late nineteenth and early twentieth centuries. Hood wrote *The French Maid* (1896) and *Little Hans Andersen* (1903), while German made a name for himself with *The Rival Poets* (1901) and *Tom Jones* (1907). Sullivan is best known for his productions *H.M.S. Pinafore* (1878) and *The Pirates of Penzance* (1879).

A Note from the Publisher

Spanning many genres, from non-fiction essays to literature classics to children's books and lyric poetry, Mint Edition books showcase the master works of our time in a modern new package. The text is freshly typeset, is clean and easy to read, and features a new note about the author in each volume. Many books also include exclusive new introductory material. Every book boasts a striking new cover, which makes it as appropriate for collecting as it is for gift giving. Mint Edition books are only printed when a reader orders them, so natural resources are not wasted. We're proud that our books are never manufactured in excess and exist only in the exact quantity they need to be read and enjoyed.

bookfinity™

Discover more of your favorite classics with Bookfinity™.

- Track your reading with custom book lists.
- Get great book recommendations for your personalized Reader Type.
- Add reviews for your favorite books.
- AND MUCH MORE!

Visit **bookfinity.com** and take the fun Reader Type quiz to get started.

Enjoy our classic and modern companion pairings!

Classic & Modern